HISTORY

OF THE

INTERNATIONAL.

Translated from the French of EDMOND VILLETARD, Editor of the *Journal des Débats*, by

SUSAN M. DAY.

With an Introduction by HENRY N. DAY, Author of "Aesthetics," "Logic," "Rhetoric," etc.

NEW HAVEN, CONN.;
GEORGE H. RICHMOND & CO.
1874.

New Haven, Conn.: The College Courant Press.

INTRODUCTION.

The conflict between labor and capital is, perhaps, an unavoidable condition of the advance of civilization. At the present stage of its progress from a state of barbarism, in which property and power belong to the few, towards a state of equality, liberty, and universal brotherhood, certainly this conflict shows itself as an invariable attendant and sign. Only under the reign of perfect virtue and good-will can the elevation of a part fail to provoke the envy, the distrust, and the ill-will of the rest. On the one side there will be instances of oppression and cruelty, which will naturally provoke resistance and revenge and lasting hate; on the other side, there will be instances of peculation and eye-service, which will as naturally provoke increasing rigor and harder exaction, and wrongs from individuals will be resented against the class. But the perfect reign of virtue and good-will is the reign of peace and contentment; only where the former is established can the latter be realized. Resistance to oppression and injustice is itself characterized by the same imperfection out of which issues the wrong it would correct or remove. The inequalities in condition, which men naturally and rightly desire to correct, exist side by side with envy and hate, which will inevitably enter into the work of reform and improvement.

It is a most worthy ambition on the part of the inferior to rise to the condition of his superior. The advance of society to a higher and better stage of civilization is impossible where this ambition does not exist; it is rapid just in proportion as this principle prevails in the community. The condition of the workman is in itself inferior to that of the employer; labor is lower than capital. It is a true and worthy manhood that seeks to rise from the one to the other. The conflict of labor and capital is not to be ended by suppressing this noble aspiration. Unless civilization recedes, the effort to rise will continue. It is rationally to be expected, also, that, by reason of human imperfection, the effort will be characterized by mistake and ill feeling; that the conflict will continue. We assume, therefore, the certainty of a continuance of the conflict; and the duty of the philanthropist is simply to seek to prevent, so far as possible, the recurrence of mistakes and the outbreak of ill-will.

No one can doubt that the interests of the capitalist and the laborer are one; that in the relation itself there is no ground of hostility, but only reason for reciprocal good-will and harmonious coöperation. Conflict arises only from ignorance, or from selfishness and malice. The two leading duties of society in respect to the prevention or diminution of the threatened evils from this conflict are obviously, first, general enlightenment; secondly, protection against wrong, and positive repression of it, so far as specific evils exist or threaten to manifest themselves.

Experience is man's best teacher. The "History of the International" is a most instructive lesson from experience. The enlightenment which we in this country, as well as the European nations, need as to the true relationship of labor and capital, and the best means of correcting and preventing the evils which are so liable to spring out of it among imperfect men, is in a rich manner given us in this instructive history. It is brief; it is lucid; it is carefully prepared; it is faithful to fact; it deals with the most stirring scenes and incidents; it traces the progress from its origin to its end of an organization of a most stupendous character, whether its principles, its advocacy, its magnitude, or its proceedings be regarded; it sets forth the strength and weaknesses of this great organization, its wisdom and its mistakes, its successes and its failure, in circumstances and conditions, too, that give it a peculiar extrinsic interest, and in the clear light of faithful narrative,—a most wonderful revelation of the workings of the human mind in regard to the most agitating social problem of modern times. It offers matter for study to the historian, the philosopher, the philanthropist; it especially brings counsel to the capitalist and the laborer alike, in regard to their duties at this present time, when society is so profoundly agitated by the practical questions which their relations involve.

In the conviction that this little history will help to solve this great problem of the age, as its solution is demanded for our own country at the present time, the translation has been undertaken, and is now commended to the favor of the public.

HENRY N. DAY.

TABLE OF CONTENTS.

History of the International.

CHAPTER I.

THE REFORMERS OF SOCIETY IN THE NINETEENTH CENTURY.

THE THEORISTS. — SAINT-SIMON. — FOURIER. — CABET.—LOUIS BLANC.

When a man falls sick, he can call to his bed of pain either a quack, who will boast of a radical cure in a few minutes, thanks to some marvellous operation, and who will finish either by doing nothing or by killing him with some drug prescribed out of place, or a true physician, who, without proclaiming himself to be an infallible savior, will conscientiously study the symptoms of the disease and fight the evil step by step, until health is completely re-established. Suffering society has also its quacks and its physicians. The physicians of the social body are the wise and prudent politicians, who devote themselves to calming passions, to subduing storms, to preventing crises, to maintaining or re-establishing peace, to bringing back equilibrium into the budget, order into the finances, liberty into the laws, in order that the condition of the whole world may grow better and better, that of each individual profiting by the general amelioration. The quacks of the political order are the reformers of great pretensions, who flatter themselves that they have found a marvellous formula, by virtue of which we will see the misery of the world vanish away, and the golden age flourish again upon the earth.

Man has suffered in all times, both as an individual and a member of society; he has very naturally sought, at all times, a remedy for his misfortunes. Unfortunately, he has been much inclined, in all ages, to lend a favorable ear to those classes who, instead of simply engaging to alleviate his sufferings little by little, promise with confidence to free him from them all by a turn of the hand. Thus, charlatans, quacks, and formers of plans for social renovation, have never lacked clients and disciples.

We will not stop to recall here all the projects of radical reforms of society, which have been carried forward by dreamers in so many centuries, some of whom were men of genius. Neither will we enumerate the different practical attempts which have been made to renovate the face of the world in a single day. We will say nothing of Plato and his *Republic*, nor of Thomas More and his *Isle of Utopia*, nor of Campanella and his *City of the Sun*, nor of Fénelon and of the *Republic of Salente*, nor of Morelly and *Le Code de la Nature*. We will not speak of the Communist movement of the sixteenth century, and of that anabaptist kingdom of Munster, whose short history offers strange resemblances to that of the *Commune de Paris;* we will not even say a word of Babeuf and his conspiracy, although there may be some likeness of descent almost direct between the *Conjuration des Egaux* and the demagogues who filled Paris with blood and flames under the third republic. But it is necessary to relate, at least in few words, the theoretical and practical history of socialism in the first half of the nineteenth contury.

The systems of Saint-Simon and Fourier were conceived by their authors and published before 1830*. But it was by means of the movement given to minds by the revolution of July, that they came out of the narrow circle of those first initiated, so as to reach the knowledge of the true public. What was their fate is well known. Saint-Simonism, embraced with ardor by a party of the aristocracy of the youth of 1830, seemed for an instant capable of converting the world; but after a period of brilliant life, it disappeared. Almost all the apostles of Ménilmontant, it is true, after twenty years of obscure efforts, reached the first ranks of industrial and financial society of the second empire, but, nevertheless, without making the ideas of their masters triumph; the dazzling fortune of the Saint-Simonians was by no means a victory for Saint-Simonism, long since dead. Fourierism, which seemed to have less chance of suc-

* Saint-Simon died at Paris in 1825, in the arms of his first disciples, Auguste Comte, Olinde Rodrigue, Bazar, Enfartin, etc.; Fourier lived until 1837, but his most important works were anterior to the revolution of July.

cess, and which never had as large a number of adepts eminent for their science and intelligence, had at least a much longer life. Retaken, resumed, and rejuvenated by Victor Considérant, as the system of Saint-Simon had been by the pleiad of his first disciples, it struggled without much glory until 1848, and seemed for a moment, after the new crisis, as if it must play, under the second republic, the rôle which its rival doctrine had filled in the early years of the monarchy of July; but it was in its turn extinguished little by little, without leaving in the world a very brilliant mark.

The first of these two doctrines completely absorbed the individual in the state, who, under pretence of directing and protecting us, became the most insupportable of tyrants. The second broke down, in a manner yet more irremediable, all personality, by suppressing not only the property, but even the life of the individual who became a simple element of a phalanx, without will, without initiative, without special rights.

These two systems at least had a singular attraction for dreamers, due to the force of the imagination of their authors, who had built the edifice of their ideal society upon a plan new and grand.

The reformers who succeeded them knew not how, any more than they, to approach the real and the possible; but far from making, like them, an appeal to the generous sentiments of human nature, they only addressed themselves to its most vulgar desires and basest passions; also, instead of attracting to them, as Fourier and especially Saint-Simon, a small number of noble minds, they ensnared merely an ignorant mob. The most celebrated of these reformers are Cabet, author of "*Voyage en Icarie*," and M. Louis Blanc, the too famous inventor of "*L'Organization du travail*." Both of these found numerous partisans, who have published the writings which we have just mentioned. "We must," says M. Corbon, in a book which deserves to be much read and quoted,* "we must distinguish the Communists determined, and consistent, from the Communists without knowing it and without intending it. These are, I am aware, numerous enough. In studying the spirit of the working class of Paris, we shall see certainly a communist tendency, manifesting itself by a marked progression towards lightening considerably individual foresight and responsibility, by burdening just as much social responsibility. Supposing that no resistance could be made to the propensity, it is very evident that one after another would arrive at the fusion of all private interests in the supreme social interest; we would have a complete community.

"But one must be very ignorant of the general dispositions of society, and even of the force of things, in order to believe that these popular tendencies can go to the final consequence.

"The decided partisans of the system were divided into two classes: the one comprised the immediate communists—that is to say, those who

* *Le Secret du peuple de Paris*, 1 vol., 8vo. 1863: Paris.

believed in the possibility of a speedy realization all at once; the other, those who, not having this belief, wished to proceed by means of transition.

"The immediate Communists were divided into two branches: the one comprising those who desired to apply the system revolutionarily to French society, the other those who pretended only to realize it among themselves, and outside of any constraint upon society. These last were ranged, for the most part, around Cabet. It was, moreover, not the Parisian center which furnished to this socialist leader the majority of his adherents; the *Icariens* were recruited from all the cities of France. The most determined went to establish a community in the southern part of the United States, at Nauvoo, a place previously occupied by the Mormons.

"The Communists of transition clung to two measures: the one of economic order, the other of political order.

"The economic measure consisted in creating social workshops under the direction and at the expense of the state, to commence by constituting it supreme director of the production and equal distributor of the products.

"The political measure consisted in advancing progressively the right of the state over private property."

M. Corbon is convinced that these deplorable tendencies were not "the fruit of the popular spirit," and that there must have been some stirring from without in order to develop them. "I have known very well," says he, "the Communist world; I have been able to follow the development of the idea; I have observed closely the work of initiation and propagation; and I shall be believed when I say that neither the initiators nor the most daring of the propagators were of the working class."

We do not propose to discuss the truth of this last assertion, but the pages we have just quoted have received a melancholy interest from the tragic events of that year. The ideas which the former member of the provisional government of 1848 believed positively judged, condemned, and even forgotten by the Parisian people, of which he boasts that he has shown us the secret, were on the contrary, even at the time at which he wrote his book, making the most frightful progress, precisely because at that time the propagators were all of the working class.

The systems of the immediate Communists of 1840 are almost absolutely known; we will study more slowly those which for three years have found their advocates in the speakers of the congress of the International, and their armed defenders in the generals and the soldiers of the Commune.

M. Corbon reminds us constantly that the *Icariens*, not finding the old world worthy for the success of their equal republic, transported themselves to America, where they hoped "to maintain themselves far from the impure breath of the old individualistic society." It is well known that after a short time the success of the experiment was such that the experimenters were obliged to settle their association by means of fire arms.

The system of M. Louis Blanc was never tried by such direct means as that of M. Cabet; but the principles on which it was formed, have been proved often enough to enable one to say that facts have, many times, confirmed the condemnation which science justly bore against them before any practical experiment.

Every one knows that the passions which inspired that detestable and fatal pamphlet, "*L'Organization du travail*," were hatred of competition and love of absolute equality. Competition, in the eyes of M. Louis Blanc, is the cause of all evils, the source of all vices; one must hasten to stop it everywhere. More competition among manufacturers or merchants excites each to produce or to sell at a better bargain than his neighbors; more competition among workmen, each endeavoring to supplant the other in the same workshop, reduces by degrees the price of their labor. Room for the social workshop, where all humanity produces for all humanity without rivalry, without jealousy; where all the workers, whatever may be their business or their function, receive the same salary; where the man of talent is the equal of the incapable; where the man of genius and the idiot are a pair; where soldiers and judges, looked upon at present as necessary in all society to prevent or punish wrongs and crimes, are replaced by a bill bearing this inscription: "The idle man is a robber." It is a complete, perfect, admirable system. It is only necessary to take care, in order to render the application possible, to commence by renovating the moral nature of man more profoundly than Fourier, in his dreams of the future, changed our bodies, those of animals, and even the constitution of the elements.

It must be confessed, besides, that M. Louis Blanc did not invent all these beautiful things. The ideas which he condensed in 1840, in his "*Organization du travail*," had been in process of formation for at least ten years, and became more popular day by day among the workingmen, as M. Corbon proves. A certain number of them found a convinced advocate, M. Buchez, who made for them too large a part in the workingmen's association, preached in 1831 and 1832 by its journal, "*L'Européen*." They even submitted to a beginning of trial, which was not favorable to them, as we shall see.

CHAPTER II.

PRACTICAL ATTEMPTS AT SOCIAL REFORM.—WORKINGMEN'S ASSOCIATIONS.

I. WORKINGMEN'S ASSOCIATIONS FROM 1830–48.

If the workingmen's association, such as we have seen organized at three different times during forty years, is an enterprise sufficiently new, yet more in the end which it proposed than in the mere practical results which it was able to attain, it must not be imagined that the workingmen had waited until the 24th of February, 1848, or even until the 29th of July, 1830, to consider that it would be advantageous for them to unite their efforts, in order to reap greater profits from their labor, and to lend in all circumstances a mutual aid. A wise and intelligent historian of workingmen's associations, M. Eugène Véron, relates that Rome had formerly its *eollegia opificum*, just as Germany aud ancient France had later their guilds. M. Corbon teaches us, on his side, that the remembrance of the corporations destroyed by the French Revolution, is dear to the working classes who still regret them.

"Since 1791," he says, "this regret has been expressed in the form of a general coalition of all bodies of trade. The laboring masses saw already the inconveniences of being abandoned, whilst the class of contractors reaped the benefits of the new system. Time has not sensibly changed the opinions of the two classes.

"As it regards the laboring masses, the regret of an institution which had in their view the character of a protector, does not always mean that the corporation dreamed of by them would be in all points organized as was the ancient one.

"However it may be, of all the systems tending to the organization of labor, that which would give a legal existence to the corporation would be the one that would best respond to the feeling of the workingmen; and I add, that wherever that institution is most vehemently desired, most peremptorily demanded, are found the workingmen in whom intelligence is most active, and who are the most ardent partisans of democratic progress."

If the corporations no longer exist, another more mysterious form of association, which was probably anterior to them, has survived them; we allude to *compagnonnage.* Without enlarging upon the fabulous origin assigned to these societies, which have had at least several centuries of existence; without giving here the history of the *Enfants de Maître Jacques,* nor that of the *Enfants de Salomon* and of the various *Devoirs;* without entering into the details of the rivalries and hatreds which have divided them, we will limit ourselves to saying that we would strangely mistake the importance of these venerable ruins of a past time, if we saw in them only simple societies for mutual assistance.

The one thought, that they are not isolated, gives to the *compagnons* a force which is wanting to the workingmen who do not consider themselves united together by a single tie; the editors of *L'Atelier*, good judges in such matters, tell us expressly :

" There is among all the workingmen who possess an organization, however imperfect it may be, a sentiment of conviction of their moral superiority over their brothers divided by egoism, separated by mistaken interests."*

M. Corbon, on his part, remarks also that wherever the *compagnonnage* exists, the workman is skilful, even if he is not a *compagnon ;* the work is relatively well done, and " the salary is greater than elsewhere," without adding that the workman is generally sound in body and mind. On the contrary, wherever the *compagnonnage* does not penetrate, the author of the *Secret du peuple* affirms that the work is poorer, and the laborer remains on a level lower than where the *esprit du corps* has preserved its ancient form.

We see that the workingmen have not waited for the creation of *sociétés de résistance,* in order to attempt, by means of a common understanding, the defense of their interests.

While corporations and the *compagnonnage* rendered formerly some services to the working classes, they must have seemed very insignificant to the ardent spirits who aspired, in the following

---

* *L'Atelier.* Dec., 1843. Page 43.

days of 1830, to renovate the face of the earth by the triumph of the most absolute democracy.

There was no attempt to protect simply the rights of the laborer against the excessive force of capital ; it was necessary to reform society from top to bottom, beginning by giving it new foundations, built upon a plan heretofore unknown.

The first architect who presented himself was a dissenting disciple of Saint-Simon, a good man, as innocent as honest, a zealous Catholic, very enthusiastic, and very ignorant of the tendencies of human nature. M. Buchez, whom we were to see, eighteen years later, president of the constituent Assembly, on the fatal May 15th, being inspired, the day following the revolution of July, with the thought of the school with which he had broken, started a monthly review, *L'Européen*, expressly to expose the miracles wich the association was to realize. His success was very great among the élite of the working class, although but very little noticed at that time by the *bourgeoisie.* If M. Buchez had contented himself with engaging the most intelligent and most industrious workingmen to unite in groups, in order to acquire little by little, by mingling their efforts and the fruits of their work, a capital which would make them dependent only upon themselves, to become patrons in their turn, he would have given excellent counsel ; but he would not have needed to be grand master of social sciences and disciple of Saint-Simon, the prophet, in order to discover so commonplace a remedy.

Moreover, there is little tendency in the French mind to content itself with truths so humble, and to trouble itself to give advice purely individual. We can only comprehend, in the matter of reforms, those who embrace humanity all together, and full of scorn of ameliorations in detail, we only deign to occupy ourselves with innovations on condition of revolutionizing all the world. M. Buchez was a true Frenchman; the readers of *L'Européen* were yet more French than he. They hastened then to conceive the first association which aspired to form the nucleus of the universal association. "It ought," says M. Corbon, who shared at first these brilliant illusions, "to be absorbing, unique, as much as possible devoted to one profession; and all, converging to the same end, should hold themselves closely bound together. In a word, we wish to constitute the community from the instrument of labor; and as the instrument of labor, in the economic language, includes machines, tools, capital moveable or immoveable, we tend then positively towards the general community of property. Our theory, at first, did not differ from that of the pure Communists, with this exception, that outside of the workshop, each disposed of his property at will."

They continued to give to associations a grand faculty of absorption; they declared then, contrary to the civil law, that they would be perpetual, and that a part of the social capital would be impersonal and inalienable. Every associate was bound to set aside a portion of his profits to increase indefinitely the impersonal social capital, and to permit the society to receive new members as fast as it increased. It should be, as it were, a lifting pump put in play, without cessation, by the devotion of the associate workingmen, and ending by drawing all the capital into the hands of the laborer; they already foresaw the day when no one could help working in order to live.

It is useless to add that labor by the job was proscribed, which took away from the activity of the laborer his most powerful stimulant, since he ceased to have in view a salary proportionate to his efforts and his skill. In like manner, also, the part of the profits which was not applied to the community, was divided among the associates according to the number of their days of work, without making any allowance for the actual quantity of work furnished by each one. Of what use is it to fatigue one's-self and make efforts by which one does not profit? M. Corbon says with exceeding reason that they had calculated without consulting human nature, which does not lend itself to such experiments. "The group of workingmen who had borrowed this plan of organization of labor, and who had propagated it as well as they could, seemed to have consciousness of the impossibility of realizing a system which demanded so much abnegation and such sustained efforts. The proof of this is that they did not make great efforts to preach by example. I know something of this. I remember perfectly that I felt and said aloud, more than once, that I should have great trouble in applying myself to such an order of things. It is unfortunate that we are always disposed to demand that others should do what we omit doing ourselves. We thought then that we had accomplished our task by propagating the ideas. If we had seriously put it in practice, the impossibilities would have struck us much sooner.*

The first association, that of the joiner workingmen, endeavored to establish itself on these bases. It was founded the 10th of September, 1831, and its statutes were compiled by M. Buchez. But in spite of all the endeavors of this celebrated man, in spite of the good will of the workingmen themselves, the society could never be established in a serious manner, and it never was really organized. Various other associations, which tried to found themselves on the same principles, had no better fortune. "One only has survived," says M. Eugène Véron, "from which we borrowed a great number of these facts, that of the jewellers, founded in 1834. It comprised at first only four associates; this number was increased at one time to eighteen; but in 1851 it fell to twelve, and to-day has only eight."† But it must have remained always faithful to the theory which it adopted at its birth. Thus M. Corbon tells us that the impersonal capital which it promised to render inalienable as far as the law would permit, was divided at the end of ten years. On the other hand, the rigorous condi-

* *Corbon, Les Écrits du peuple de Paris.* 2d part, chapter II.

† M. Véron's book *(Les Associations ouvrières)* appeared in 1865.

tion of its constitution made a close circle for it. Thus this association, which should have absorbed all the laborers of the universe, found itself, at the end of thirty years, modestly reduced to eight members. Yet M. Véron remarks with much justice, that if it had prospered in spite of the errors of its statutes, it was explained by the character of its associates. "They are," he says, "men profoundly religious, who find in the exaltation of their belief a compensation for the moral stimulants which they have thrown away. This is why they are resigned to remain in a state similar to torture, while the association prospers and the community is enriched. One sees very well that this cannot be proposed as a model for other associations, which cannot be entirely composed of saints.

II. WORKINGMEN'S ASSOCIATIONS UNDER THE SECOND REPUBLIC.

We have seen only a small number of workingmen's societies established during the reign of Louis Phillippe, but the theories which made the association the remedy of all the evils of the laboring classes, and the force destined to regenerate the world, were never so much in favor as at the time when the Republic triumphed for the second time in France. On the 25th of February the association was inscribed in a decree of the *Hôtel de ville,* beside the guaranty of labor. The Constituent Assembly did not leave off promising the signature of the provisional government on this point, and July 25th, 1848, upon a report presented by M. Corbon, the assistant editor of *L'Atelier*, it voted a law opening a credit of three millions, designed to furnish advances to the workingmen who wished to become associated. At the same time, there was instituted a council of encouragement, to examine the demands and regulate the conditions of the loan. Ten days later the Assembly took a new step in the same direction ; the workingmen who had united themselves under certain fixed conditions, were admitted to the adjudication or even to the direct concession of public labors ; they went so far as to dispense with the security required of those who undertook the trust. Among the associations which took advantage of the privilege of this second law, one alone, that of the pavers, was an actual success, and realized great benefits simply by procuring an administration for the city of Paris.*

The council of encouragement instituted by the law of the 5th of July, devoted itself to the work and published a pamphlet, where was found yet more of the ideas of the editors of *L'Atelier* than those of the majority of the Assembly, for it spoke of the duty imposed upon the Assembly " of assisting, by the means of which it could make use, to remove laborers from the condition of receiving wages to that of voluntary associates." As we can readily believe, clients were not wanting. The council received more than five hundred de-

* Levasseur, *Histoire des classes ouvrières en France, depuis 1798 jusqu'à nos jours*, Book 5, chapter IV.

mands in 1848, and more than a hundred in 1849; not merely three millions were needed, but thirty and more, in order to satisfy all those who presented themselves. "The chest was opened," says M. Levasseur in his excellent *Histoire des classes ouvrières,* "many imagined that they had only to draw from it. Workingmen became associated without any determined end except to receive aid, or with pretensions that could not be realized, and vague aspirations. Patrons whose affairs were embarrassed, associated their workmen in order to have a right to the loan of the treasury." They did what they could by cutting down their parasites, and after a choice difficult enough to make, they finished by admitting thirty-two associations in Paris and twenty-nine in the departments, by a total of 2,945,500 francs—that is to say, nearly the whole of the credit; some resignations and reductions reduced the amount actually loaned to 2,590,500 francs, divided among fifty-six sssociations.

In the month of March, 1850, *L'Atelier* appreciated the spirit which inspired these societies, in an article in which we find some interesting information.

At the time when the revolution of February broke out, there were, according to this journal, in the socialist party, four very distinct groups. That of the pure Communists, which had for its organs *Le Populaire* of Cabet, and *La Fraternitè* of MM. Adam, *cambreur,* Mallarmet, worker in bronze, Savary, etc., condemned formally the association;

the three others, on the contrary, expected to see in it the grand instrument of social regeneration; only they wished to organize, the one according to the principles of the phalansterian school, the other according to those of M. Louis Blanc, the third according to the conception of the editors of *L'Atelier*.

If we are to believe the article which we are now analysing, the greater part of the Communist workingmen abjured, after February, their contempt of the association, and were only desirous of changing their condition of receiving salaries into that of voluntary associates.

Notwithstanding that the movement impressed all minds by the revolution which was just accomplished, one association alone wished to regulate itself upon the laws of the Phalanstery. Projected in 1847, it endeavored in 1848 to establish itself upon a domain situated some leagues from Paris, and it was disappointed. "The socialism of Fourier," says the editor of *L'Atelier*, "is propagated but little except among young scholars; the popular social element remains almost a stranger to this doctrine. So that of the three constituent elements of the phalanstery, the school has only found one, *talent*. *Capital* and *labor* have been wanting in order to try thoroughly the theory of integral association."

The system of M. Louis Blanc was, on the contrary, very popular with the laboring classes; most of the associations wished to conform to it; many even imagined, in the highest faith in the world, that they followed religiously its laws ; but *L'Atelier* has no trouble in showing that they only deceived themselves :

"M. Louis Blanc only conceived of the association as a means of destroying competition. We have seen him fight with all his energy and with all his eloquence against the thought of distinct associations, divided in interests, especially when there was concerned but one single profession.

"That which M. Louis Blanc wished, was an association unique and tending to become universal. He only admitted the material division of the labor of workshops and localities. But he wished that all workers should sink absolutely their particular interest in the ccmmon interest, and that they should conform to the law of most complete solidarity.

"According to the doctrine of M. Louis Blanc, there should be, wherever there was need of them, social workshops; here of joiners, there of tailors or of masons ; in fact, there would only be one and the same association which should be the nucleus of the universal association.

"As for the principle of repartition. it should be that of the strictest equality.

"This destruction of competition by community of interest in all social workshops, and equality of salaries, are the two great conditions of M. Louis Blanc's system. Take away these two conditions, or one only, and the whole system falls to the ground.

"Now the one hundred and eighty workingmen's societies which were established in Paris, under the symbol of a level,* are they only different workshops of one and the same association?

"No. Except three or four associations which have one or two dependencies, or three at most, each associate group forms a group perfectly distinct and perfectly separate from the others.

"Some efforts were made and renewed for the consolidation of workingmen's associations: these efforts failed. The establishments which had the courage and perseverance to surmount all the difficulties of founding do not seem in the least disposed to make common their cause and treasury with other establishments more or less well organized.

"As for salary, most of the associations in their origin, wished it to be equal, conformably to the theory of M. Louis Blanc. They were almost all obliged to renounce it.

"Thus the two fundamental conditions of M. Louis Blanc, those which alone characterize the system which he himself formed, that is, unity of interest and equality of salary, have failed completely in practice.

"Competition, for which M. Louis Blanc had a horror which all his adherents shared, is made use of among the associations.

---

* The number of 180 societies given by *L'Atelier*, compared with the number of 32 associations, admitted for Paris, to take part of the 3 millions voted by the Assembly, proves that the number of societies which were created without aid of the Government was infinitely greater than is generally believed.

"It is made use of even in the bosom of association; for salary proportionate to the work, as quantity and as quality, is still competition.

"We are then perfectly justified in saying that the transformation which begins to operate by means of the association, proceeds no more from the theory of M. Louis Blanc than from that of the phalansteries."

However, the co-workers of *L'Atelier*, while demonstrating that victory remained to their own ideas, recognized in the author of *L'Organizatiou du travail* the merit of having energetically pushed the workingmen into the path of association. If his personal theories failed, it is because the force of circumstances and human nature itself condemned them. We see by the acknowledgments of M. Corbon, in *Le secret du peuple de Paris*, that the editors of *L'Atelier* who no longer shared in 1848 the errors of M. Louis Blanc, had at least in former times paid them tribute; if they were undeceived while M. Louis Blanc still believed them, it was because they were thrust into practice, while the noted publicist always remained in the domain of theories.

Meanwhile M. Corbon and his friends were themselves amused in 1850 by many illusions, and at the moment in which they spoke with exultation of the transformation which had begun to operate by means of associations, the societies upon which they grounded so much hope were almost all on the brink of destruction.

Cruel miscalculations were truly not slow in

chilling the beautiful enthusiasm of the earlier days. Incompatibility of humor among the associates, mobility of character, want of skill, absence of a voluntary discipline to replace the enforced discipline of ordinary workshops, finally, above all, the incapacity of most of the managers, and the dishonesty of some, brought into the societies which were just established, numerous revolutions, and caused much ruin. In 1852, among the fifty-six associations created by means of the funds voted by the Assembly, there were counted thirty* which had foundered swallowing up together nearly one million. In 1858, in Paris there remained only nine of the thirty-two of the associations which had profited by the agreement of the State, and of these nine societies only four prospered. Of the hundred and eighty associations cited with pride by *L'Atelier* in 1850, there only remained ten in 1867. M. Levasseur, from whom we have borrowed these figures, adds:

"The statistics mention less than fifteen hundred workingmen, who attempted, with or without the public assistance, to become associated, less than three hundred who with difficulty persisted until 1852, and this indicates that the capital accumulated by the associations, in six years, remains still inferior to the supply furnished in 1848 by the State.

"It is, in short, a small result. What are some hundreds of thousands of francs earned by fifteen or

---

* 18 in Paris and 12 in the department. They had received 954,000 francs in loan.

twenty groups of ten or twenty persons by the side of fortunes realized, in the same lapse of time, by old workmen becoming manufacturers or contractors? If it were possible to make a list of salaries in 1848, which in a period of ten years have changed conditions, and to place in comparison the profits amassed by those under the régime of individual activity and under the régime of cooperation, the part of the latter would assuredly appear little worthy of fixing the attention of history.

III. WORKINGMEN'S ASSOCIATIONS UNDER THE GOVERNMENT OF DECEMBER.

The imperial government showed itself in its commencement but little favorable to the workingmen's societies which had lived until the 2nd of December. Disposed to see everywhere elements of conspiracy, it suppressed most of those which had survived, societies of production, of consummation, or of mutual aid, without distinguishing very much the object which they had proposed. But, after some years, the notion of association, which had appeared dead, acquired all at once a new force, and ended by being as favorably received both by the *bourgeoisie* and the government itself as the laboring elasses.

The experience of 1848 had profited. They no longer demanded from the state a patronage which had come to be regarded as more hurtful than useful. There was little or no question of equality of salaries ; the workingmen—those, at least, who were in the associations,—comprehended that capital is an indispensable element of production, and they recognized that it was just, when necessary, to give it its part of the fruits of a labor which could not have been accomplished without its aid. Capital, on its part, no longer seemed afraid of associations. In 1863, M. Béluze founded in Paris the *Société du Crédit au travail,* which had for its aim "the crediting of associations actually existing, and the aiding in the formation of new associations of production, of consummation, and of credit." This society, which ended by breaking down in later years, seemed for an instant called to play a rôle as blessed as important. Numerous societies of production were created with its aid and capital ; it received funds, to a great extent, of mutual credit, it discounted the paper of a great number of coöperative societies, and was rapidly aggrandized itself, for, during the three first years of its short existence, the number of its associates and the amount of its capital had increased tenfold. MM. Léon Say and Walras founded, on their side, the *Caisse d'escompte des associations populaires,* which prospered rapidly, and the emperor, seeking to favor now the movement which his government had violently combatted in 1852, gave 500,000 fr. to constitute a *Caisse des associations coopératives.* In the departments, five or six treasuries of the same nature were formed between 1864 and 1867 ; M. Levasseur mentions among others the *Société lyonnaise de crédit au travail,* the *Banque de crédit* *au travail* of Lille, and the *Crédit populaire* of Colmar. In the last half of the year 1866, there were already counted in Paris, one hundred and twenty *crédits mutuels*, seven societies of consummation, fifty-one societies of production ; and in the departments, one hundred societies of natures differing in function or in formation.*

They believed for a moment that they were assisting, not, indeed, in the commencement of the universal renovation dreamed of by the socialists, but in the first period of a revolution, peaceful and deep, which would effect, little by little, commerce and industry. It was a mistake. The movement, which seemed as if it must acquire new strength every day, soon loitered, and without having produced either a commercial or political crisis, most of the societies, which had seemed just now on the point of wholly conquering, disappeared, one by one, and quietly made settlements more or less disastrous. It would be impossible for us to say how many had subsisted till the last year at the time of the declaration of war, but we have reason for believing that the number was very much reduced.†

---

* Levasseur, *Histoire des classes ouvrières.* Book 6, chap. VI.

† At the complementary elections of July 2d of that year, those associations which still existed, published a very moderate manifesto, designed to oppose abstention ; it closed thus : " Whom shall we choose ? before all, the men of rank who wish to maintain the Republic. What have we to gain from revolutions ? Nothing. What have we to gain by the maintenance of order and of the Republic ? Everything. Come then to us ; observe carefully our candidates, and then : To the ballot ! It is the only weapon of honest citizens and laborers."

Nearly all were wrecked upon rocks signaled in advance by men of good sense, to whose wise counsels and sad but verified predictions they refused to listen.

We do not wish, neither are we able, to examine here, one by one, all the obstacles which rendered, truly not impossible, but very difficult the success of these associations; yet there is one main thing which we think useful to notice in this preface to the history of the International, because this obstacle belongs to the passions which have most

---

"A committee of initiative of the workingmen's associations." This placard, which persuaded the electors to apply "to one of the delegates, 10, Rue Mayran," was printed by the new printing house (a workingmen's association), Rue des Jeûneurs, 14, at G. Masquin and Comp.

Another placard, printed by *L'Association générale typographique, Rue du Faubourg, Saint-Denis,* gave a "list of the Republican candidates of the workingmen's associations, of the employés of industry, of commerce, and of administration." This list contained only five names, placed in the following order:

MM. Cohadon, founder and manager of the coöperative Society of Masons; Mamy (Jules), manufacturer; Mumeaux, founder and manager of the coöperative society of spectacle-makers; Dreux, founder and manager of the coöperative society of locksmiths; Pioche (Joseph), director of the coöperative society for the consummation of the union of agricultual and industrial factories; founder and president of the council of inspection of the coöperative society for the production of cabinet ware and furniture.

Below these names were two lines which merit notice as a sign of the moderate ideas of these candidates and their patrons. "To attain this end—just coöperation of labor and capital." It would be interesting to know just how many votes were given to the representatives of the coöperative associations; but the journals have not told us this.

powerfully aided in the formation, in the development and the formidable success of this execrable society.

When an association is established, not with the purely negative aim, to propagate hatred and war, but with a positive aim, to produce and sell its products, it is not sufficient to have working arms, it is necessary that there should be a head to direct their efforts : the work must be divided among the workers ; the work, when finished, must be examined in order to see that it is well done ; tools must be bought, and materials, without any mistake as to quality or price ; it is necessary to employ those who will make products of a nature satisfactory to the consumers ; as soon as they are fabricated, markets must be found for them ; one must know how to sell them to men who can honor their signature, if one is forced, as is generally the case, to accept in payment, not cash, but notes to mature in longer or shorter time. It is necessary, then, that he or they of the associates who are to play this rôle of direction and control, possess a mass of information perfectly useless to those who only furnish to the society the work of their hands. These directors, or, to call them by the name that the notion of equality and some little jealousy among the associates consented to give them, these managers who should have more instruction, more intelligence, more taste, more delicacy of mind, more subtlety of character than their comrades, under penalty of misfortune to the society and of ruin to each of the associates, shall they only be, as regards rights of all kinds and daily renumeration and share of the profits, the equals of those men to whom they should be superior in almost everything? At most times this question would have been resolutely answered in the affirmative; but as the force of circumstances is superior to all the decisions of a society, whatever it be, the associations have found it almost an impossibility to find capable managers under such circumstances, and when it has not been internal want of discipline which has killed them, they have perished by being badly directed and badly administered. When, on the contrary, they consented to give to the chiefs they had elected the right of commanding and of directing with sufficient liberty; when, at the same time, they have accorded to them pecuniary advantages a little in relation to the degree of intelligence and of knowledge of all kinds which they were obliged to possess, they became so quickly the object of such lively jealousy, that the exercise of their functions was soon rendered impossible.

The force of circumstances furnished in the presence of this great question of ruling, three or four solutions, almost all equally disagreeable to the workingmen who were united in the hope of arriving speedily at freedom without having thenceforth any superiors. In most cases, want of discipline among the associates and incapacity of the managers brought about, more or less rapidly, ruin; in other cases, a small number of associates became able, thanks to the retiring or lassitude of the others, to transform themselves into veritable patrons and conduct more or less ably an enterprise upon conditions almost resembling those of the mills founded and directed by the *bourgeoisie.* Sometimes a manager, at the same time incapable and dishonest, precipitated the final crisis by disappearing some fine night with the remains of the joint capital. Finally we even see some of these republics transformed absolutely by a stroke of authority into absolute monarchies. Thus the association cf chair makers, founded in 1848 with some four hundred members, and reconstituted in 1849 after numerous internal rendings, with only twenty associates, still suffered numerous vicissitudes during several years. At last, a little after the 2nd of December, the manager, M. Antoine, possessed himself of absolute authority: "Well! yes," said he to a German, M. Huber, who visited France and England in order to study coöperation, "yes I have made my little *coup d'état* as well as another. And why should I not have made it, since they turn out so well, these *coups d'état*? That we must do in all things, as other Frenchmen do to us, is a good and powerful command." Let us add that a long time before the hero by whom he regulated his conduct had led France as far as Reischoffen and Sedan, the dictator of the chair-makers was compelled to disappear, and that his disappearance was accompanied by circumstances little edifying.

In a country much less favorable to *coups d'état*, in England, M. Huber found also some managers who had known how to impress their power upon their former equals : the history of one of them is most interesting, and we shall be pardoned if we give up to him a few lines.

There were, a long time ago, in London (this authentic history begins like a fairy tale), seven brothers, all gigantic, named Musto, who were all machinists. The eldest, William, a good speaker and distinguished agitator, placed himself one day at the head of a strike, into which he very naturally drew his six brothers. After a certain time, one of them, John, seeing all the family resources wasted, firmly decided not to re-demand work from his "patrons," but, understanding on the other side the absolute necessity of returning to business, proposed to others to associate themselves and to work on their own account. He had read some numbers of the "Christian Socialist ;" he had been taught by some friends already embarked in the coöperative movement, and some philanthropists of Lincoln's Inn, what had given to him, thanks to his natural penetration, a sufficient idea of the aim and means of the societies then new. With his brothers, except the orator William, and two or three of their companions, by realizing their last resources and contracting a little loan, they collected a hundred pounds sterling, and formed a workshop. But the affair did not progress ; each one wished to command, and no one was willing to obey ; customers did not appear, credit vanished. Then John Musto addressed his associates : "How can you expect," said he to them, "that people will trade with you, when they do not know who has the charge of affairs? People, you know, have to do business with some one person. Moreover, they always find us quarreling and arguing instead of working. It cannot go on so, and, for my part, I will not consent to it any longer. Do you wish me to tell you what is the matter? There is not one among you capable of directing affairs, and how can you expect to do it all together? Now I can direct, and you know it very well, and if you do not give me full liberty, all will be over between us. *I will make my way all alone.*" Thus the brave John Musto made his *coup d'état*, and he laughingly told M. Huber that, by way of peroration to this eloquent speech, he showed a pair of muscular fists.

Some time after, the coöperative society engaged the associations protected by it, to respond in writing to various important questions submitted to them. It asked of them, among other things, to what cause each association attributed essentially its success, and what recommendation their experience would consider most important for future associations. The associate mechanics of London responded: "Place the control in the hands of a small number." It is to be believed that this time John Musto had no need, in determining this answer, of the eloquence of his famous fists.

Let us add that this society, established in 1852, with 2,500 francs, in part borrowed, possessed, in 1854, more than 70,000 francs. It is true that it disappeared in 1857; but it succumbed to a crisis which carried away, at the same time, a great number of individual enterprises, and its fall proves nothing either against the principle of association, or against the necessity of intelligent control entrusted to one man or a very small number.

John Musto, in his memorable speech to his associates, pronounced a profound saying, upon which we cannot reflect too much, because it sufficiently explains, on the one hand, the small success of most all the associations; and, on the other, the immense number of adhesions received in a few years by the International. *I will make my way all alone.* This is precisely what constituted the power of most of the manufactories, mills, banking and commercial houses conducted by the *bourgeoisie.* It was because the same force of circumstances placed at their head only those men sufficiently instructed and intelligent to *make their way all alone,* as the men who thought themselves strong enough to *make their way all alone* did not care to share the profits to which they had the right to pretend with a crowd of associates, who would aid them, it is true, by means of their small capital, but who, by want of intelligence, by ignorance, or even by most fatal jealousy, would fetter all their operations and constrain all their movements. When a man is capable of becoming the real and true head of a great exploit, which he can direct in all freedom, and of which he can receive the profits, either entirely, or at least in a very large proportion, can he be contented in exercising in an association a power uncertain, precarious, insufficient, and without being recompensed for his trouble except by receiving a part of the profits scarcely superior to that of the least of the associate workingmen? For this, one must be a hero, a saint. Now, heroes and saints are rare in all times and in all countries.

On the other hand, there is an immense multitude of workers who, not feeling these exceptional faculties, know in the depths of their hearts that they are wholly incapable of *making their way all alone*, and who have seen perish, moreover, one by one, most of the associations upon which they had counted for the realization of their long cherished hopes; this multitude, we can believe, were very ready to rally about men who promised to lead them, promptly, by ways apparently less arduous, to the satisfaction of their long awakened desires, their eternally unappeased appetites.

IV. COALITIONS.—STRIKES.—SOCIETIES OF RESISTANCE.

Long before the first of the societies, of which we have just related the history, was founded, there were created associations of an entirely different character, which have played a great rôle in the economic world. We speak of coalitions. The coöperative society is a permanent association which has for its aim, production, after that, the division of the fruits of common labor: the coali tion is an association generally temporary, formed in view of war, sometimes offensive sometimes defensive, between labor and capital. During the early days of our great revolution, coalitions were, in Paris, one of the greatest anxieties of government, and the constituent Assembly did not hesitate to repulse them by law, for it feared to see renewed, under this new form, the corporations it had just suppressed*

The penal code was possessed of the same mind, and forbade the coalition, that is to say the design however pacific it might have been, whether of the workmen to refuse their labor on the conditions offered by the employers, or of the employers to diminish the salaries of their workmen. But this law, seeming to take equally the part of both sides, was very easily eluded by the masters who, few in number, could readily write and have an understanding, while the workmen, by reason of their large numbers, could not come to an agreement without noisy and tumultuous reunions which themselves seemed to draw down the intervention of justice.

Few years passed under the Restoration, in which the tribunals did not judge one or more cases of coalition : the number of affairs of this kind increased considerably under the monarchy of July, not that the laws were more rigorous for the workmen on strikes, but because the elevation of the price of everything, and the increase of public fortune, rendered more necessary than under the preceding régime, advancement of salaries, to which the employers cared very little to assent. We can

---

* The history of these coalitions will be found in the book already quoted of M. Levasseur, Book 1, Ch. II.

form with the collection of *L'Atelier* a complete list of condemnations to which this kind of crime has given rise since 1840. The number is frightful. These processes, to be regretted from a natural point of view, were from a political point of view inconvenient in the first degree. Every time that an affair of this kind made a little noise, the government press raised its voice against the workingmen, the organs of the governmental opposition maintained generally a discreet silence, and the cause of the "laborer" was only sustained by the radical sheets *Le National* and *La Réforme.* Then the workingmen, who for the most part even then held themselves aloof from any political tendency, passed with arms and baggage,—with arms especially,—into the ranks of the revolutionary party. Thus the government made many enemies, whom it met in the street, gun in hand, on the 24th of February.

The provisional government did not pass a law for abolishing the articles of the code which forbade coalitions: it contented itself with not applying them. During the year following, we see that they had entirely fallen into disuse.

"Since 1849," says M. Levasseur* "coalitions have been numerous, some of them blustering. The tribunals prosecuted each year, with power, seventy-five coalitions of workingmen, eight of employers, and pronounced more than four hundred condemnations. There were often found in these

* *Histoire des classes ouvrières.* Book vi, chap. III.

trials the same scenes of violence as under Louis Philippe." However, scarcely were these condemnations pronounced by the tribunals, than the emperor granted, or even gave without being asked, pardon to the condemned. It had, to use the very just expression of the ministers in a confidential report, "neither the advantages of a penal legislation enforced with rigor, nor the honor and advantage of a liberal legislation." It was therefore decided to amend the articles 414, 415, 416 of the penal code, by establishing a distinction between simple coalition, which was permitted, and coalition accompanied by violence, by culpable manoeuvres, by blows for the rights and liberty of employers or of workingmen, which was punished severely enough. This law, which was prepared by M. Emile Ollivier, and the discussion of which excited a lively interest in all places, was voted in the session of 1864; the same rules to-day over such matters. Every one remembers the immense strikes which were produced almost immediately, and the violence, deeply to be regretted, to which many of them gave rise. Some months after the passing of the law which authorized coalitions, the International Association of Laborers was founded in London; from that moment most of the important strikes were either prompted or at least aided by it. But before entering into the very heart of our subject by showing the International at work, it remains for us to say a few words about certain societies which were, so to speak, its cradle.

All the facts which we have here related are established in a sure manner by official documents;

the history of the associations of production has already been given; it would be easy to continue it by taking the accounts from the journals and public acts. The history of strikes would also be very easy to write, since each of the incidents of the contest between capital and labor has left marked traces, which can be found in the publications of the workingmen and of the employers, in the books of the economists, and in the archives of the tribunals. But there is a history which can only be made with great difficulty; it is that of the permanent societies organized by workingmen, either in view of resisting all encroachments of employers, or of taking the offensive, in their turn, and obtaining increase of salary or reductions in the time of labor. We know that in France no association can be formed without the authorization of the government; now, no one of the governments which have succeeded in France could authorise the formation of a society formed to organize war between employers and workingmen. Societies of this kind have, nevertheless, existed for many years; but they have managed it, either by carefully hiding themselves and living in the condition of a secret society, or have disguised their true end by designating themselves societies of mutual aid, of professional instruction, of reading, etc. But the administration ignored, or seemed to ignore, these clandestine reunions. No trial has revealed the existence of the society, which ended either by dissolving or disappearing, or in being merged in a larger society, without having left in any public document any trace whatever of its existence. Formerly, a political trial or a case of coalition permitted one to guess, even to affirm, the existence of one or more of these offensive or defensive leagues ; but their members denied it with energy before the tribunal, and the historian may fear, that to his affirmations resting upon an attentive study of the facts, there will be opposed anew these official denials of most interested witnesses. We can only indicate here the general movement of the associations. The printers of Paris were, we believe, the first who were thus united. The aim of their union was primiitively, only to defend themselves against all attempts at reduction of salaries. It is useless to add that, very soon, they passed from the defensive to the offensive. Other workingmen of the same class leagued themselves similarly, not only in Paris, but even throughout France. Afterwards these societies, at first isolated, understood the interest which they had in uniting in a mutual understanding and supporting each other. In this manner, the groups, at first not very numerous, and without any tie between them, became gradually enormous and compact masses, whose force seemed at certain times irresistible. They were extended not only among several neighboring professions in the same city, but in neighboring cities, afterwards with analogous groups in the most distant provinces. It only remained to establish a connection with the workingmen situated beyond the frontiers of the country. We will proceed to see what circumstances led the French associations to pass the boundary.

CHAPTER III.

TRADE UNIONS.

PRACTICAL SOCIALISM IN ENGLAND.—CRIMES OF SHEFFIELD.—TRADE UNIONS.

The general conditions of existence for the different classes of society, are, in this century, sufficiently similar in nearly all the nations of Europe, to make us certain that the social and political passions which we find in any one of them will be found almost identically the same in all the others. These passions may express themselves by phenomena a little different in appearance, according to the special temperament of the people, but their general character is everywhere the same, at bottom ; before all study of facts, then, we have reason to suppose that in the country whose economic conditions approach most nearly to ours, we shall find in the head and heart of the laboring classes almost the same ideas, prejudices, desires, and hatreds, that we have just verified among the French workingmen. When we observe what is happening, not only in Belgium and Switzerland, but also in England and Germany, we see that this conjecture is just, and that the same causes have produced the same effects north of the British Channel as south, upon the right bank of the Rhine as well as upon the left bank.

Since the first revolution, a certain number of foreigners have played a great part in all our excesses, and, without official commission, have represented their countries in the saturnalia of the demagogues. We will only mention the most celebrated of these representatives of international rashness, the Prussian Anacharsis Clootz, who was called the orator of the human race, and who had the honor of leading to the *Champ-de-Mars*, at the fête of the Federation, a grotesque assembly of the scum of all nations, intrusted with symbolizing the fraternity of the people.

We called to mind, at the close of the preceding chapter, the coalitions and strikes which appeared in France at the beginning of the Restoration, that is to say, as soon as the re-establishment of peace permitted us to return to work. Industrial life was not suspended in England by the contests which imbrued all Europe in blood, during the Revolution and the Empire, far from it; also the activity of industry had there developed the war of labor and capital, and the armies of workers were organized to protect it. The workingmen's societies destined either to resist the pretensions of the employers, or to attack them by dictating laws to them, were already numerous in 1824, when it had been decided, forty years before us, no longer to punish coalition as a crime.

M. le comte de Paris, in his fine work on the workingmen's associations in England, which he published in Paris, in 1869, expresses himself thus; "For forty years the English workingman has enjoyed the liberty of coalition, of disposing of his labor as of his merchandise, as the producer of his products. To-day the army of workingmen enrolled under the banners of the Trade Unions can rival that of the larger states of the continent, for it is composed of eight hundred thousand volunteers. Even among its adversaries, no one expects its dissolution ; for this, it would be necessary to go violently backward, even to the laws which formed the bondage of the working classes. It must then reckon upon a force as numerous and as well organized, and the interest of all classes would desire to pursuade it to lay down arms, by showing that it could find better employment for its power than in the barren conflicts in which it has been engaged until now."

We share, unqualifiedly, upon this point, the wisely liberal opinions of *M. le comte de Paris:* but it must be added that the conversion which he is so anxious to bring about is not the most easy. To what a degree are the hearts of one part of the soldiers of this army embittered, what stores of hatred can they treasure up, to what extremities can these men little educated and passionate be driven, it is this that the English forget to-day too easily, though a famous inquest may have revealed it to the world.

There is, indeed, no one who has not been shaken by terror upon hearing this year of the crimes by which the Commune has signalized its agony. But we must consider that the wretched people who have crowned by such crimes their bloody career, were over excited for two months and a half by a war without hope, that for more than six weeks the incessant noise and each day nearer approach of the cannonade must have driven even to the most furious madness, the folly which led them into an enterprise as extravagant, as criminal. The English, who seemed too often in their journals to render all France responsible for those fires and murders, ought to remember the crimes with which certain leaders of the workingmen of Sheffield were stained, without any circumstances which could account for their madness. Since they forget so quickly, we are permitted to remind them of them.

There existed in Sheffield, as in all other industrial cities of England, a great number of workingmen's associations, whose chief aim was to sustain strikes, but which, at Sheffield as elsewhere, sought to exercise, at the same time, an absolute influence upon their industry, to impose all their wishes upon the employers, to subject all the workingmen to their slightest caprices, and by this to oblige them all, without exception, to be united with them. Whoever refused, was immediately in their eyes an enemy against whom everything was permitted, his resistance must be broken at any price. In order to punish and intimidate those who were refractory, their tools were secretly hidden, and they were subjected to a thousand vexations which only ceased, when, tired of the contest, they decided to submit. As for those who allowed themselves to retire from the society, no punishment was too cruel for them. During the space of fifteen years, many of these "renegades," in Sheffield, were assassinated, struck by a mysterious bullet issuing without noise from an air-gun. Others had their houses destroyed by the explosion of powder boxes placed in the cellar with lighted matches; their families ran the risk of being destroyed by them. During nearly fifteen years, these crimes were frequently repeated, and fear made the independent workingmen understand that they must submit to the tyranny of the societies or perish. An inquest, opened by a commission of Parliament, closed by discovering all the truth concerning these crimes and by making known, in all the details, the mournful history. We knew of what the compatriots of those humane and pious editors of the English journals which seem to attribute to-day to the French the privilege of a native ferocity, were capable, in perfect peace, and without the excitement of war.

However, we must not fall into the error and injustice which we condemn in others. As the immense majority of Parisian workingmen are innocent of all complicity in the crimes of the *Commune* of Paris, in the same way the majority of the *trade unions* must not be rendered responsible for the crimes of Sheffield, and we must examine the organization of these societies without prejudices against them.

"The *trade-union* is preeminently," says *M. le comte de Paris*, "a permanent treasury for slack seasons. After having generally paid an admission fee, sometimes pretty large, the members pay each week a subscription varying from one penny to one shilling, and even in certain cases, two. A reserve fund is thus formed, which grows rapidly in prosperous years, and which is destined to sustain the members of the society when they are at at a stand still, either from lack of work, or in time of a strike. The subscription is equal for every member, and this equality is one of the bases of the institution, for it implies an equal aid in case of stoppage of work; in time of a strike, it does not matter whether a workman earns much or little, the union must keep him from starving.

The society is ruled by a council of inspection, an executive council, elected each year by the secret vote of all the members, and which comprises in its midst a president, a cashier, and a secretary. The government of the society, the relations with employers, the decisions relative to strikes, the distribution of indemnities, finally, the striking out and admission of members, belong to this council exclusively. To the general assembly are reserved the grand financial affairs, such as the imposition of an extraordinary contribution upon all the members, if, one part of them being on strike, the normal resources of the society do not suffice to sustain them.

"But the most powerful unions, as the united mechanics, the united carpenters and joiners, the masons of the two large societies, the workers in iron of Staffordshire and of the north of England, the weavers of Lancashire, the national association of miners, which numbers 35,000 members, and still many others, have a more complicated organization, and are themselves divided into a great number of branches. Each branch or lodge is composed of workingmen living in the same district, chooses its committee, has its special treasury, which it administers, but of which it must give an annual reckoning to the central council. This is formed of delegates elected for six months by the different branches, proportionally to the number of their members, and of two employés, the secretary and the treasurer, named directly by the suffrage of all the members.

"There are lodges which admit into the union the candidates presented by two members, and which decide in the first resort concerning exclusions, aid, and local strikes. But one can always appeal to the central authority, and the lodge which makes a strike without having obtained the sanction of this authority will not be sustained by the society. Finally, the vote of taxes and the appeal of a lodge against the decision of the council, belongs to the general assembly.

"Although the treasury of slack seasons always plays the principal rôle in the administration of the unions, a small number only among them, called by way of distinction *trade-societies*, limit the use of their funds exclusively to the aid of strikes. These societies are generally of little importance. Others offer besides, to their members, certain advantages borrowed from societies of mutual aid, such as a weekly indemnity in case of accident, and almost always in case of sickness, the expenses of burial, amounting to 200 or 300 francs, and often half of this sum for the funerals of their wives. Some insure them against the loss of their tools, and there are three which guarantee a retreat for the old and infirm."

We have endeavored to make known, practically, the organization of the *trade-unions*, because it resembles, in many points, as we will see later, that of the International. For the same reason we have dwelt upon the coalitions and strikes in England, because it was in England that this society was organized, and which has even to-day its general council. We will say almost nothing of Germany, because, though the Germans have entered into the International, they have contributed much less to its establishment than the French and English workingmen. However, it will suffice to recall the names of Jacobi and Lasalle, to prove that socialism has had its teachers as well in Germany as in France. Moreover, everyone knows that the socialist press is larger and more powerful among our enemies than ourselves to-day. As for those of our readers who desire to know about the most serious practical attempt at social amelioration which has been made on the other side of the Rhine, we we would recommend the book of M. Seinguerlet upon the *Banks of the people of Germany*. They will find there an instructive and complete study of these institutions of popular credit, which have made famous the name of M. Schultze Delitzsch, their founder.

Until these later years, there had been no personal relations between the working classes of the different countries of Europe ; when *L'Atelier*, edited by the workingmen of Paris, wished to make known to its readers the movements of coalitions and strikes in England, it was obliged to give them analyses of the articles which M. Léon Faucher had just published on the subject in the *Revue des Deux Mondes*. We ought to notice, it is true, a strike of tailors in Paris, wnich was sustained for an instant by money sent from England. It was in 1840, at the time when the question of the East menaced France with a war against all Europe combined, and the Parisian strikers were spiritedly reproached for having sought aid from the enemies of their country. *L'Atelier* responded to this reproach. "The letters of advice state that this money comes from their brothers in London ; it is honorably acquired by them ; it is the offering of the laborer to the laborer, and not the price of an ignoble subsidy, at the idea of which we all revolt."* We have found in the whole collection of this journal, which we know appeared until 1850, no other traces of facts of this kind, and for a long time the coalitions of laborers in each country found neither aid nor even response in neighboring countries.

Two sayings paint vividly the change which has taken place in a few years, in this respect, in the economic relations of different powers.

Léon Faucher said, in 1849, that England could support coalitions because it had commercial liberty.

In the book published twenty years later, by *M. le*

---

* 1st number of *L'Atelier*, September, 1840, page 4.

comte de Paris, we read this phrase which is plainly the counterpart of the assertion of Léon Faucher: "When the English manufacturers reproached their workingmen with ruining industry, with ruining themselves in demanding an increase of salary which favored foreign competition, they responded that the workingmen of the Continent would soon obtain in their turn the same increase, that they would aid them, if it was necessary, and thus the parts would be again equal."

How had the situation changed so completely in twenty years? How had that which was very true in 1849 become absolutely false in 1869? It is because personal relations were established between the workingmen of different countries; it is because they had agreed to abolish competition between them, and to declare, on the contrary, war against their employers. It is because the International was born.

CHAPTER IV.

FOUNDING OF THE INTERNATIONAL.

I. THE LONDON EXPOSITION OF 1862.—THE FETE OF THE INTERNATIONAL FRATERNITY AT THE TAVERN OF THE FREE-MASONS.

The first idea of the founding of the International Association of Workingmen has been often attributed to Mazzini. It is a mistake against which the members of that society have vehemently protested with various repetitions, who, notwithstanding their love for overturning, have perhaps as much hate for the revolutionary *bourgeoisie* to which the celebrated Italian agitator belongs, as for the conservative *bourgeoisie.*

We have seen during many years, that workingmen's associations more and more vast have been established in broad daylight in England, where the law permitted them to be founded and to live ; in secret or under some disguise, in France, where the associations are subject to the régime of preliminary authority. It remained only for these societies, already so powerful in their respective countries, to pass over the straits in order to be associated together.

The universal Exposition at London, in 1862, furnished the occasion which they needed ; every one, on that side of the channel, assumed the most innocent ardor in facilitating the journey to the French societies.

On the 29th of September, 1860, the *Progrès de Lyon*, advised the workingmen to tax themselves, in order to permit their delegates to go and admire the marvels of the great industrial congress which was being prepared in London. M. Arlès Dufour found the idea excellent, and made haste to declare that the Imperial Commission "would neglect nothing in order to obtain from the railroad companies the greatest facilities and prices exceptionally low," in favor of these interesting travelers.

L'Opinion nationale very much hoped that the example set by the workingmen of Lyons would influence all the grand industrial and manufacturing centers of France: "The visit," said this journal, "which our laborers would make to their comrades in England, would establish among them relations profitable to all in all respects; at the same time they could observe for themselves the great artistic and industrial works which are to be seen in London, they would be better sensible of the solidarity which binds them, the old leaven of international discord would be quieted, and the rival jealousies would make way for the salutary efforts of a fraternal emulation." Consequently *L'Opinion nationale* rallied with all its heart about the idea, expressed by *Le Temps*, of opening a national subscription, for paying for the delegates of the great manufacturing centers the expenses of the journey already greatly reduced by the intelligent assiduity of the imperial government.

On every side, the matter was made so attractive to the future travelers, that a Lyonese laborer did not delay writing to the *Progrès de Lyon* that he suspected a trap:

"When the initiative comes from above," said this doubter, "from superior authority or from employers, it only inspires workingmen with moderate confidence. They think or believe themselves directed, conducted, absorbed, and the best endeavors are rarely crowned with success."

It must, nevertheless, be added that, in this case, "success" has answered much more to the desires of the suspicious correspondent of the democratic sheet, than to those of M. Arlès Dufour, of the Emperor Napoleon III, and of the editors of *Le Temps* and *L'Opinion nationale.*

A project so ardently favored by every one at the time, could not fail of success, and the delegates, almost all chosen by their comrades, as must have been expected, in the party most advanced and most passionate of the working class, arrived safely at London, upon a pleasant summer's day in 1862.

Thus far we have not had occasion to verify up to what point they considered well, as they had been expected to do, "the great artistic and industrial works" which figured in the galleries of the Exposition, but they were wonderfully sensible of "the solidarity which binds them," and "the old leaven of international discord," which had not been for a long time very dangerous, was very quickly replaced by the leaven, entirely new, of social discord, whose marvellous energy we can admire at this moment in our streets in ashes.

It would, however, be a mistake to suppose that the delegates departed from France with all the savage passions which the society that they were to establish nourishes to-day. It would be an equal mistake to suppose that they found in England these passions, pushed to the degree at which we see them now ; no, the careful study of all the documents proves a fact, moreover, profitable in itself ; it is, that in the International as in other political institutions, and even in certain national assemblies—in the Long Parliament, for example, or in the Convention—individual passions, already violent, became more bitter and more terrible by continuous contact ; that men the most intelligent and the least carried away were borne down by the less intelligent and more violent, who found themselves immediately, in their turn, surpassed by a new flood of madmen for whom they themselves were too calm and too moderate. Many of the first French founders of the International have refused to lend themselves to the excesses of their successors ; they pass to-day in their eyes for renegades, and if they have not been treated as the *Girondins* by the *Montagnards*, it is because the Commune has not endured long enough, and has not extended its power far enough to sacrifice all the objects of its hatred.

But let us return to London and the Exposition of 1862. On the 5th of August, " the fête of the international fraternization," all the delegates were assembled at the tavern of the free-masons. The English workingmen read there an address to their brothers in France, which has come to us almost entire, thanks to the different fragments which M. Murat quoted before the tribunal of the Seine, during the suits brought against the International in 1868 and 1870.

This address is sufficiently interesting for us to reproduce here all the passages these two speeches give us:

"We, English workingmen, have seized with joy the occasion of your presence in London, to extend to you a fraternal hand, and we say to you with all our hearts: You are welcome.

"In the ages of ignorance and darkness, we have only known how to hate; then was the reign of brute force. To-day, under the shield of civilizing science, we meet as children of labor; the reign of moral force has come. . . .

"Although the future seems to promise the satisfaction of our rights and of our hopes, we ought not to disguise that we will not arrive there without serious contests; egoism renders men too often blind to their true interests, and produces hatred and derision where there should be only love and union.

"In the same manner that our national dissensions have been ruinous to our respective countries, our social divisions will be fatal to those whom competition influences against their brothers.

"As long as there are employers and laborers, as there is competition between employers, and disputes concerning salaries, union among workingmen will be their only means of safety.

"Concord between us and our employers is the sole means of diminishing the difficulties by which we are surrounded.

"The improvement of machines, which we see increasing on all sides, and the gigantic production which is the result of the application of steam and electricity, change every day the conditions of society. An immense problem is to be solved, that of the remuneration of labor. According as the power of machines increases, there must be less need of human labor. What will be done with those who are without work? ought they to remain unproductive and as elements of competition? Should they be left to starve, or fed at the expense of those who work?

"We do not pretend to solve these questions, but we say that they must be solved, and that for this task it is not too much to demand the concourse of all: of philosophers, of statesmen, of historians, of employers, and workingmen from all countries. It is the duty of every man to take part in this work.

"Many systems have been proposed for the solution of this problem; most of them have been magnificent dreams; but the proof that the truth has not been found, is that we are still seeking it.

"We think that by exchanging our thoughts and our observations with the workingmen of different nationalities, we shall discover most quickly the economic secrets of societies. Let us hope that now as we have clasped hands, as we see that as men, as citizens and as laborers, we have the same aspirations and the same interests, we shall not permit our alliance to be broken by those who believe it for their interest to disunite us ; let us hope that we shall find some international means of communication, and that every day will form a new link in the chain of love which shall unite the laborers of every country."

In this address, which is, so to speak, the instrument of the birth of the International, there are found without doubt, certain errors, certain illusions ; but the tone of it is suitable and moderate, it does not appeal openly to violence, and it does not even seem as if brute force was the power upon which the compilers of this address, in the depths of their hearts, placed their hopes. But there is one thing worth noticing, (for it is a sign of the course which the ideas of the International Association followed fatally), it is that only the most moderate passages of this address were quoted by M. Murat in the first trial ; the paragraph relating to the utility of concord between the employers and workingmen, and that in which appeal is made for the solution of certain problems to the concourse of employers and workingmen of all nations, had been read before the tribunal in 1868, they were struck out in 1870, without doubt in order not to lose from the society numerous adepts whom these sage ideas would have revolted ; and moreover, M. Murat is in the International, a kind of *Girondin*, almost a renegade. By the course which he had gone over in two years, judge of the progress which the anti-social passions had been able to make in the same time among the *Montagnards* of the association!

After having listened to this discourse, the French delegates, through Mr. Melville Glover, their interpreter, expressed their desire to see committees of workingmen established, "for the exchange of correspondence upon the questions of international industry." This proposition was received with warm applause. Such was, according to the recital made by M. Murat to the tribunal, the origin of the society whose history we are studying.

There is every reason to believe that the actual truth is very near the official truth; it suffices probably to replace the beautiful scientific terms of *questions of international industry* by the more practical words of rates of salaries, of opportunity for strikes and means of sustaining them.

To speak plainly, the workingmen of the two countries were convened to establish between them a permanent understanding upon all questions of salaries and coalitions: there remained for them to find practical means of realizing it, a durable form must be given it, a fixed organization to the association whose utility they had just recognized, and its principles set forth. This was the work of two years. The imperial commission, in its inexhaustible solicitude for the workingmen to whom it had furnished the means of going to London* to ac-

* "The advanced republican party wished to draw us; we resisted it like the rest, and then, as we had obtained aid for the

complish this brilliant task, had, without doubt, taken the precaution to furnish each of its protegés with tickets for going and returning. They did not all have to use their return tickets. "Many delegates," says Murat, "found themselves *advantageously situated* during their stay in London. There ensued an exchange of letters, which increased, from day to day, the need of constituting a common center of correspondence."

We have the right to intrepret the words of the accused, reciting to a tribunal the facts of an affair in which he was implicated. It is, then, lawful to suppose that the *advantageous situations* found by certain delegates, were solely or principally, the aid which their brothers and friends had promised them, in order that they might remain in England, to work in the vineyard of the Lord. To drop a biblical metaphor, little in keeping with such bad christians, it was to be their especial work, (Murat acknowledges it almost directly,) to collect the necessary information in order to see in which of the two countries, in what part of each country, and in what branch of industry, there would be the greatest advantage in beginning the war, in organizing vast strikes, whose success would be assured by the moral and material concourse of all the associates. Only, the more the delegates, remaining in London in their advantageous situations, were occupied with the question, the more would they recog-

---

journey to the London Exposition, it happened that we were called Bonapartist agents." (Defense of Murat, third trial of the International Association of Workingmen, published in Paris, in July, 1870.

nize the necessity of an organization, vast, solid and permanent.

The following year, it was necessary to reunite; there was no longer need of the universal exposition nor the eager concourse of M. Arlès Dufour and the aid of the imperial commission. A pretext was found in a manifestation in favor of Poland, which was organized or was found already organized by unconscious god-fathers. It was necessary to pay for somewhat dearer places in railways and steamboats and to pay for them themselves; this did not prevent six new Parisian delegates from hastening and arranging with the organizers. There is every reason for believing that, in this reunion, the definite principles of the association were determined: but the existence of the society projected, and especially the execution of the projects in view of which it was organized, were yet very difficult in France, with the laws which existed at that time. They did not despair of modifying this inconvenient legislation, and the facts soon proved that it would have been wrong to despair.

II. THE QUESTION OF THE WORKINGMEN'S CANDIDATURES IN PARIS IN 1864.—LAW CONCERNING COALITIONS.—MEETING AT SAINT-MARTIN'S HALL.—PROJECT OF STATUTES OF THE INTERNATIONAL.

Some general elections had taken place in France in the spring of 1863. By reason of the double nominations obtained by several of the chiefs of the opposition, there was occasion to nominate two deputies from Paris in the month of March, 1864. While the leaders of the left and the extreme left disputed about the choice of the candidates whom they should propose to the electors, there suddenly appeared a manifesto signed by sixty workingmen, who demanded that one of the vacant seats should be reserved for a "laborer." The sixty signers, among whom we notice, with other leaders of the International, MM. Tolain (graver), Murat (mechanician), Limousin (lace maker), and Camélinat (worker in bronze), did not hesitate to perplex politics by laying down suddenly the social question :

"Universal suffrage," they said, "has made us great politically, but it remains for us to emancipate ourselves socially."

Then followed the inevitable tirade against the enemy, towards whom, especially, the growing society proposed to declare war :

"Those who, destitute of instruction and *capital*, cannot resist by liberty and solidarity the egoistic and oppressive exigencies, suffer fatally from the domination of *capital*."

In consequence they demanded, first of all, the abolition of the articles of the code which forbade coalitions ; but they sought to reassure, at the same time, the electors and deputies as to the consequences of such a reform :

"To those who believe that they will see resistance and strikes organized as soon as we claim liberty, we would say : You do not know the workingmen ; they pursue an end much greater, much more fruitful than that of wasting their forces in daily contests, in which on both sides the adversaries will find nothing definite but ruin for the one and misery for the others. The third-estate said: What is the third estate? Nothing! What must it be? Everything. We will not say: What is the workingman? Nothing! What must he be? Every thing! But we will say: The *bourgeoisie*, our elder brother, knew, in '89, how to absorb the nobility, and destroy unjust privileges. It remains for us not to destroy the rights which the middle classes justly enjoy, but to obtain the same liberty of action. . . .

"Let us not be accused of dreaming of agrarian laws, chimerical equality, which would place each one on the Procrustean bed, distribution, forced taxes, etc. No! It is high time to stop these calumnies, propagated by our enemies and adopted by the ignorant. Liberty of labor, credit, solidarity,—that is our dream. In the day on which it shall be realized, for the glory and prosperity of a country which is dear to us, there will no longer be *bourgeois*, nor proletaries, nor employers, nor workingmen. All citizens will be equal in rights."

They made haste finally, in order to tranquilize the republican *bourgeoisie*, to declare that they wished, as it did, for universal suffrage relieved from all fetters, liberty of the press, liberty of reunion, complete separation of church and state, equilibrium of the budget, municipal franchise. "What do we desire more especially than they," they added, "or, at least, more energetically, because we are more interested? Primary instruction, gratuitous and obligatory, and liberty of labor."

Aside from the railing against capital, we see that the wishes of these signers were presented in a manner the most modest, we were going to say the most encouraging. We could say of socialism as did Dorine de Tartufe: "*Alas! how sweet it is; it is all sugar and honey.*"

However, the *bourgeoisie* would not be seduced; immediately another manifesto, also signed by a certain number of workingmen, blamed the untimely pretensions of M. Murat and his friends, declaring that it was no time for submitting workingmen's candidatures, and that it was not necessary to complicate the political question by a social one. The sixty, nevertheless, persisted in their opinion, but their candidate, M. Tolain, could only get in the fifth district, where he presented himself, 380 votes.

This check seemed destined to discourage the party which had dreamed of conquering the world by means of the society in prospect of formation; but, if some discouragement entered at that time, which, indeed, is not certain, into the soul of M. Tolain and his friends, it must soon have given place to lively hope when the discussion of the law concerning coalitions came before the *Corps législatif.*

M. Emile Ollivier, who had just been associated with the empire, was charged with the defense, in the character of a reporter, which brought upon him, very naturally, instead of the thanks of the workingmen whose cause he pleaded, the most violent attacks, and the names of traitor and apostate. A fraction of the chamber, which had especially for its spokesmen MM. Seydoux and Kolb-Bernard, opposed the project, as they considered it dangerous for society. The extreme left, on the contrary, combatted it, by the voices of MM. Jules Simon and Jules Favre, as incomplete and insufficient. Echoing the sentiments of the majority, M. Buffet saw the defects of this law, but judged that it would be still more inconvenient to reject than to adopt it. "By rejecting it," he said, "we would not have destroyed the evil that we dread; we would only have driven it inwards and made it more dangerous. Now, in this situation, I consider it a duty, notwithstanding my doubts, notwithstanding the anxieties of my mind, to adopt the entire project."

Thus, in spite of the opposition of the extreme right and the extreme left, together with the coldness of the centers, the law was adopted by 222 voices against 36.

Coalitions were from that time authorized in France. The vast association projected within two years received from the hands of power and of the *bourgeois* opposition, aid without which it could have done nothing in France. It hastened immediately to be definitely constituted.

On the 28th of September, 1864, the "English workingmen" convoked at London, in Saint-Martin's Hall, a grand international meeting which three French workingmen attended, "delegates from a little group to which some of us belonged," says Murat in his defense before the imperial court.* There, were arranged the provisional regulations of the International Association, or rather there were ratified those which the actual leaders had brought prepared, there, was named the committee, or rather the powers which these same organizers had taken upon themselves were validated, finally it was there that the correspondents for the different countries, represented in the meeting, were designated by means of election.

The provisional statutes settled by this meeting were those which, two years later, the members of the first universal congress of the International adopted, exaggerating, only, by some additions, the violence of the ideas ; they deserve then to arrest us a moment.

The first thing which these compilers of the statutes declared in their considerations was, that "the emancipation of laborers must be the work of the laborers themselves." No idea, without excepting perhaps their hatred of capital, entered more passionately into their heads and hearts. Also, in the different suits which were brought against them later, we see all those inculpated have declared by turns, that a very great wrong and almost an injury was done to them in attributing to Mazzini the first idea of their society :

"And to say," cried Chalain in the third trial, "that,—we know not with what intention,—you make

---

* Audience of April 22nd, 1868.

of Mazzini the founder of the International! We have proclaimed sufficiently, moreover, that we no longer wanted deliverers, that we no longer wished to serve as instruments, and that we had the pretension to have knowledge of the situation, to understand our interests as well as any one." Truly, nothing is more praiseworthy than to wish to do one's own business one's self, and to reckon upon work and not upon the aid of others in order to free one's self. It is an excellent sentiment; we do not desire that the workingmen shall renounce it; we only wish that they might come to have a clearer view of the reality, to understand that they can *serve as instruments* quite as well to the ambitious from among their own ranks as to the ambitious of other classes, and, moreover, to better distinguish their true interest than many of them have done to this day.

The first consideration of the committee chosen at London, in 1864, exposes the necessity for workingmen to emancipate themselves.—The second entertains us—it was inevitable,—with the misdeeds of the bugbear, to which it is the custom to-day, among the working classes, to attribute all the evils of humanity, as the royalists of 1815 attributed them to Voltaire and Rousseau. "Considering that the subjection of the laborer to *capital* is the source of all political, moral and material servitude."

Then comes the grand remedy, the new panacea which has held such a place for ten years in the ordinances of all the doctors of socialism, solidarity: "Considering that all efforts have failed, for want of *solidarity* between the workingmen of different professions in each country, and a fraternal union between the laborers of different countries."

The following considerations only developed the necessity of that famous solidarity destined to regenerate humanity ; they ended by recognizing the necessity of founding an International Association of laborers.

All the members of this association and all those who wish to join it, "should recognize that Truth, Justice, Morality, should be the base of their conduct toward all men, without distinction of color, belief or nationality."

Perhaps the compilers of these statutes believed that they had made a great discovery and realized an immense progress in proclaiming as the rule of their conduct, truth, justice, and morality. However, no society has ever considered itself placed under the protection of injustice, falsehood and immorality ; every one has a most beautiful desire to conform to the true, the just and the good. The misfortune is that there is great trouble in precisely agreeing upon these principles, and that, for example, the immense majority of French, English, Germans, Italians, Spaniards and Russians obstinately regarded as false, unjust and immoral, most of the principles admitted as articles of faith by the International in its later congresses. The compilers of these statutes have then taken much trouble for nothing, and their discovery is much less precious than they imagined.

To these declarations of principles and declamatory or chimerical generalities succeeds the practical part, that is to say a sketch, still vague and confused, of the organization of the future society. The principal point is the establishment of an annual general congress, which shall have the office of a constituent and legislative assembly, and which will nominate the permanent grand council, destined to be the actual government of the society.

They urge, moreover, the associates to use in their respective countries all their efforts "to reunite in one national association, the different existing societies of workingmen, also to create in each country a special organ."

Finally, not to frighten and discourage any one, they were careful to recognize, in a concluding article, that, "although united by a fraternal bond of solidarity and coöperation, the workingmen's societies would, none the less, continue to exist upon the principles which were peculiar to them."

Thus, in the theoretical part, grand declamatory phrases and false ideas, but, unfortunately, very well calculated to attract a suffering and little enlightened mob. In the practical part, dispositions very well contrived, and a first element of organization skilfully enough conceived to offer grand chances of success; this is the résumé of the work of the first committee of the International.

It is, truly, already a society little worthy of encouragement, and we see too well of what passions it made use, and what passions it tends to develop. However, it must be acknowledged that there is a great difference between these ideas, fatal as they are, and those which the exultation of first success hastened to develop among the greater part of its adherents.

III. HISTORY OF THE INTERNATIONAL ASSOCIATION OF WORKINGMEN BETWEEN THE BANQUET AT SAINT-MARTIN'S HALL (1862,) AND THE CONGRESS OF GENEVA (1864).

It had been arranged, at London, that the first annual congress should take place the following year, that is to say 1865, at Brussels.

While waiting for this great day, the organizers of this association, on their return to their respective countries, devoted themselves with ardor to their work of propagation.

The want of success of the manifesto relative to the workingmen's candidatures in 1864, and the positively ridiculous number of votes which M. Tolain had received, gave reason to suppose that the new society would be recruited with much difficulty in France, or at least in Paris. This was a superficial and inconsiderate judgment. Thanks to the demoralization which the spectacle of the scandalous fortunes of the heroes of December and the total absence of political liberty, had spread in the population of the large cities, and especially among the working classes, the success of the preachings of the International was unhappily too well assured.

Moreover, as we have explained above, almost

all the working population, especially that which labors in large work-shops, was already enlisted in the very numerous associations, of which some existed in broad daylight under some pretext of study or mutual benefit, while the others, who had not deigned to resort to these disguises, lived in obscurity, perhaps not ignored, but tolerated by the administration. Thanks to this organization, the conversions effected by the missionaries of the International could proceed not by isolated individuals, but by compact groups. A bureau opened No. 44 *Rue des Gravilliers* received the adhesions and the subscriptions. Everything was transacted in broad daylight, and the opening of this bureau was even announced in the journals of the month of January, 1865.

In his speech before the tribunal of the police magistrate, during the trial of the second committee of the bureau of Paris, a man who was to play one of the chief rôles in the Commune, Varlin, teaches us that the year 1865 was almost entirely consecrated to this propagandism. "The International Association," says he, "had to make itself known. Its progress was slow at first; however, after existing some months, it counted in Paris a sufficiently large number of adherents to cause belief that the idea had been understood, and that it would make its way. A sub-committee, composed of workingmen belonging to the different professions, was formed in order to aid the correspondents in their task, and especially to prepare the congress which was to take place. It was in truth urgent that France, which had conceived the association, should be worthily represented."

However, this congress, for which such active preparations had been made, did not take place. Varlin, who is not bound to tell us "the truth, the whole truth, and nothing but the truth," because he did not appear before the tribunal as witness, but as accused,—Varlin pretends that if the reunion was countermanded, it was in order to punish the Belgian government for having just "re-imposed its law upon foreigners." The association, not finding Belgium worthy of showing it hospitality, persisted in not assembling there, in order to "affirm loudly in the face of all Europe the absolute right of reunion, as it had affirmed in France, by constituting itself, the natural right of association."

We easily perceive the real fact which is concealed under these grand words. It is very clear in truth, that if, in order to *affirm*,—to follow the new jargon of the demagogic party,—the right of association, it must become associated, the best way which could be found of *affirming* the right of reunion, would be to re-unite.

Moreover, if Belgium ought to be punished for a measure which its government had taken, the founders of the International preserved, in every case, the resource of transporting their *affirmation* into England, where no law had been imposed or re-imposed upon foreigners.

The truth, disentangled from the International phraseology and the mania for *affirmations* of the citizen Varlin, is, in all probability, that propagandism had not, at the close of the summer of 1865, produced sufficient effect to warrant trying, with serious chances of success, a general reunion. Nothing could be more sure of cooling the growing zeal of the catechumens, than to find themselves in a hall hardly filled, where few of the different nationalities would be represented.

The general congress was replaced by a general conference, held at London, at which only the initiated were present, from which the profane were religiously excluded, and where one could speak with the greatest freedom among intimates. They did not fail, as that was necessary, to announce pompously in all the journals, that they had received tidings of the formation of numerous groups in Germany, Switzerland, Italy, Denmark, and Belgium. After a little time, these conquests were actually effected, and they had contributed not a little to their success, by announcing them in advance as accomplished. Is not this, in the development happily nigh at hand, the game which Varlin and his friends were to play in 1871, when they changed every morning, in their official journal, the defeats undergone by their troops the night before into brilliant victories won by the confederates?

The conference at London was closed, always according to the same historian, by a festival which celebrated the anniversary of the founding of the association, and the delegates separated naming Geneva as a rendezvous, where it had been decidedly chosen to hold the following year the first congress.

Varlin continues by enumerating to us the principal deeds of the International:

"In the course of the year 1866," he says, "it showed itself in a most conspicuous manner apropos to the military events of which Germany and Italy were the theatre.

"It was not political, but it *affirmed* strongly the social principles which directed it.

"It opposed the right of labor to the right of arms; it placed the alliance with the commonalty above the enmity of the governments.

"And finally, in the month of June, it opposed the economic programme of the congress of Geneva to the political lucubrations of the cabinets.

"It prepared the public, by publications almost weekly, for the grand reunion which was to establish in a definite manner the International Association, up to that time in a provisional state.

"In the month of July following, it made known to its adherents, always by means of the journals, the efforts made in the country for the constitution of new bureaus.

"In the month of September, 1866, the congress of Geneva took place. Seventeen French delegates presented themselves at this reunion, where the fundamental compact was debated and voted.

"The Association existed this time in a definite manner; it entered into the practical road."

The friends of the International will not complain that we have represented unfaithfully this part of its history, since it is from one of the fathers of its church, that we have borrowed it literally.

Now, in order not to divide up our history needlessly, and to place alone in one chapter the history of the four councils, we mean of the four congresses in which the new faith was elaborated, we will proceed to expose the organization of the democratic and social church. We can do this so much the better because this organization was not created but simply confirmed by the congress of Geneva.

CHAPTER V.

ORGANIZATION OF THE INTERNATIONAL ASSOCIATION OF WORKINGMEN.

I. THEORY AND PRACTICE.—SECTIONS.—FEDERATIONS.—BRANCHES.

Up to this time the writers who have treated of the International and described its organization, have too easily confounded on this subject the theory and the practice, the rules and the manner in which they were enforced.

It is, however, necessary to distinguish, apropos of all societies in general, between the provisions written in their statutes, and the manner in which they are applied.

It is still more necessary to make this distinction in judging of the International.

Let us first consider the theory.

A larger or smaller number of members of the association grouped together, either because they belong in the same country to the same body of trade, or more simply, in other cases, because they inhabit the same city or same locality, form a section. Several sections of the same region form a federation. All these federations united compose the association which is directed by the annual congresses and governed by the general council. The members of each section choose from among themselves the delegates who are to represent them, some at the federal council, others at the congress. The congress, in its turn, elects the members of the general council, whence it follows that the association is always in theory, administered from a government sprung from an election of two gradations.

In practice, it seems that things have occurred in a precisely inverse manner. The founders of the society seemed to have constituted from the beginning the general council, whose powers have been simply confirmed by the pretext of an election by the four annual congresses which have already been held. Finally, as far as it is lawful for us to conjecture in such matters what takes place in the heart of a society to which we do not belong, and to which we have never had the slightest wish to belong, it is likely enough that in a number of cases, without doubt in the majority of them, the delegates of each section are the active and enterprising men who formed it, by grouping around them an unimportant nucleus of catechumens.

An example, which all the Parisians who assisted at the first siege are acquainted with, will illustrate our supposition.

We know how a large number of battalions of the national guard were formed after the 4th of September.

A small number of ardent revolutionists, in general all associated with or members of the International, (and it is this fact which renders our hypothesis infinitely probable,) united themselves, distributed among their friends nearly all the epaulets, from those of the commandant down to those of the second lieutenant; then they sought out in the neighborhood some hundreds of simple people, whom they persuaded in one way or another to join the new battalion. Each one believed simply that the elections had been made before his enlistment, but that he only obeyed after all the officers chosen by his comrades; in reality, he found himself enrolled, although he was there without suspecting it, in a corps, equipped solely by the revolutionary party, in view of a war to be declared some day against society, and not of the actual conflict with the Prussians. As the mass of men thus enrolled were ignorant of politics, indifferent and easy to lead, the battalion was very soon won by the party of social revolution. When, by chance, they had to do with an honest and intelligent majority, it finally freed itself, but with some trouble, from the sorry fellows who had organized it. It was thus that Sappia, who was to perish in the insurrection of January 23rd, was, early in the month of October, 1871, arrested by his battalion, whom he wished to lead to the assault of the *Hôtel de ville.*

It was thus also that Varlin, who had possessed himself of the command of the 193rd battalion, was finally deposed during the siege, thanks to the energy which the honest men who composed the immense majority of that corps displayed in opposing a chief whose antisocial ideas and behavior disgusted them; only they had the greatest trouble in freeing themselves from that commandant who pretended to have been chosen by themselves.

In the International, accidents of this kind were not to be feared, and the ringleaders, who had formed a section or federation, have been until now, as we have reason to suppose, almost sure of remaining as its delegates. Officially, their authority comes from it; in reality, it has only existence through them. The brave, honest men who let themselves be duped by these ringleaders, believed that they gave an impulse, by their votes, to one of the grandest forces which existed at that time in Europe; in reality, there were hundreds of thousands, millions of poor devils, who were so many puppets of whom the ringleaders pulled the string, and the too probable suspicions respecting certain relations of Assi with the chiefs of Bonapartism, prove sufficiently that this immense army could, at a given moment, be led in a body to battle, not only in a cause of which it was ignorant, but even in the interest of the men whom it most violently hated.

To return to the organization of the International, the associates form the first, the elementary groups called *sections*. Certain sections, in consequence of peculiar circumstances, remain isolated; but, ordinarily, the sections of the same region are formed into one *federation*.

Although the principle of the International is the annulment of nationalities, nevertheless the same force of things has led to embracing all the federations of the same country under the name of a *branch*.

All the *sections*, all the *federatious*, all the

branches, taken together, constitute the International Association of Workingmen.

II. LOCAL COMMITTEES.—FEDERAL COUNCILS.

Let us pass now from the associates to the different councils which they represent.

Several sections near to each other, too small to form a federation, unite to constitute a *local committee*, which serves as a medium between them and the federal committee. When these sections are numerous enough in one region to form quite an important group, they constitute a federation. In this case, each section sends its delegates to the *federal council*, which serves at the same time as a medium between the different sections, and between the sections and the general council.

"This council," says M. Oscar Testut, "is charged with the defence of the salaries and the different interests of the corporation, and the consideration of economic and social questions; it must endeavor to establish a union between all the workingmen in their struggle against the *farmiug of the capital.* It is bound to make an active propagandism among the working classes, to explain to them the principles and the end of the International, to initiate them into its organization, to lend them its aid when they wish to be formed into regular societies, and to furnish them for that purpose with necessary directions.

"Every month the federal council is obliged to send to the general council a statement of the situation of the federation, and a report concerning the administration and the financial condition of the sections situated in its jurisdiction.

"It is this also which decides upon the demands for loans addressed to the federation, upon the opportunity for sustaining strikes, obtaining loans from an adherent society, or from the general council, of sending delegates to the congress, of admitting or refusing the associating of a new society, etc., etc. It is charged, moreover, with enforcing the orders of the general statutes and the decision of the congress; all the communications emanating from the general council are addressed to it, to be read to the different members, who are in their turn to make them known to the corporations, of which they are the delegates.

"The constitution and the composition of the federal council varies according to the importance of the localities, and the larger or smaller number of the working classes federated."

Most localities do not possess a federal council. They are only established when the multiplication of the sections renders its formation necessary in order to have a common center of action.

When a federal council exists in a locality, it alone corresponds with the general council by means of a corresponding secretary. Two collective letters addressed in 1867, the first to the different democratic journals, the second to the *Journal des Débats*, by M. M. Tolain, Varlin and Fribourg, who all signed themselves at the same time in the capacity of *correspondents*, give us reason to believe that these *corresponding secretaries* have also in their province the relations of the society with the press.

Have the different federations a common center in each country? This is hardly to be doubted, and as for France, in particular, we have only seen too well with what unanimity the society obeys the word of command.

However, it does not seem that one sole center, belonging to each nationality, has everywhere an existence openly recognized. Thus, while we see that there is in Belgium a *general Belgic Council* which is the central point whither all the federations of the country lead, the magistrates under the empire charged with drawing up the three charges against the society, could not find, among so many important papers which they had seized, but one which authenticated the existence of a supreme council for all France.

The new edition of the work of M. Testut contains a document, until now unpublished, which is of the greatest interest upon this question. This is a copy:

REPUBLIC, DEMOCRATIC AND SOCIAL.

DELEGATION.

The federal council of the Paris sections of the International Association of Workingmen, and the revolutionary delegation of the twenty *arrondissements* of Paris, delegate and give full powers to citizen Albert Leblanc, member of the International, and of the executive committee of the delegation of the twenty *arrondissements* of Paris, to be respected by the sections of the International and the revolutionary groups of the province.

PARIS, FEBRUARY, 1871.

For the federal council
of the International Association
of Workingmen:
HENRI GOULLÉ,
Secretary.

For the delegation:
CONSTANT MARTIN,
Secretary.

It seems then, according to the amplest information obtained from this paper (evidently of the most secret character, consequently very well suited to reveal to us the truth), that the French branch of the International has not a special superior council named by all the federations, but that the federal council of Paris has over the other federations and sections of the country, a supremacy accepted in reality if not recognized by right.

It is possible, however, that the papers seized since the fall of the communist insurrection give us full light on this point. The debates which have been opened at Versailles before the councils of war cannot fail to enlighten us upon some points yet more obscure.

III. GENERAL COUNCIL.—CONGRESS.

However this may be, the local committees and the federal councils, whose provinces we have just made known, lead to a common center, the general council, the seat of which was, in theory, to be designated by the congress for the following year, but which, in fact, had been from the first, established at London, where the society was founded, and seemed as if it would remain there always, unless some events hardly probable should oblige it to be removed.*

"The general council," says M. Testut, "should present at each congress a public report of the doings of the year, it should establish relations with the different workingmen's associations, examine the questions which are submitted by the sections, and decide if there is a general interest in what is to be discussed at the next congress.

"It is charged with the organization of the congress, and, to this end, it must publish in advance its programme, and make it known to all the sections by means of their corresponding secretaries.

"Every quarter, it is bound to make known the state of the working classes in all the countries, the situation of the coöperative societies, the size of the salaries, the adhesions which they have acquired, the strikes which have broken out, the results obtained, etc. To this effect, a written communication is addressed to the secretary of each section: it is reproduced in the journals of the International.

"There appears a fact of an important nature to compromise the future of the association, and to change its character; if it concerns the attacks directed against it or a great blow to be struck, the general council publishes the manifesto, of which many thousand copies are struck off, translated into all languages and scattered in profusion in all the working centers. These manifestoes conclude with this formula: *In the name of the general council*

* M. Testut tells us that the bureaus of the council are established at 256 High Holborn, London.

of the International Association of Workingmen, and are signed by all the secretaries."

The council is charged with collecting all the documents which are communicated to it; "the duty devolves upon it of executing the resolutions of the congress. It is judge of the disputes which may arise between the sections or members of the International Association, reserving appeal to the next congress; it always decrees after a report presented by a jury of honor."

This general council is,—at least officially,—named each year by the congress.* In fact, since the founding of the society, its composition has not varied in a very sensible manner, and the men who know how to have themselves elected are always those who had the first notion of the association, who have created it, and who hold it in their hands at their personal distribution, perhaps even, in certain cases, at the disposition of some great leader, discreetly kept in the shade, whose secret plans the innocent mass of associates accomplishes probably,

---

* In the very instructive book of M. Oscar Testut, from which we have borrowed so much, we find a passage which shows us how the founders of the International understood maintaining their friends or their creatures in the important posts of the society. We can judge by this that they were no more at a loss how to maintain themselves:

"The 9th article of the general statutes gives, it is true, to each section the right of naming its correspondents; but this power exists only with certain restrictions. In theory, when one section is in process of organization, it is the general council which confers upon a member already affiliated with the International, the title of correspondent; the section once organized, this choice is always ratified by the adherents."

at certain times, without suspecting whom it is obeying.

The workingmen of Creuzot little knew, in the beginning of 1870, what grudges they were satisfying and what political intrigues they were serving.

The confederates of 1871, of whom many, without doubt, still loved their country, although joined to the International, did not ask themselves if the insurrection, whose success made them so proud, was not by chance seen with joy at Berlin, if the revolution of March 18th was not a new victory for Bismarck. The destroyers of the *colonne Vendôme* did not dream that the ropes attached to the monument which recalled our victories over Germany, had, perhaps, been placed there at a command from beyond the Rhine. As soon as the Commune had conquered, the Germans, who, after having served in it, sought refuge in the Prussian lines, were immediately shot. We are certain that they will no longer betray any secrets,—Molière had already remarked the perfect discretion of the dead.

This digression must not take us too long from our subject. Let us hasten then to return to the general council.

We have related how it is chosen, according to the text of the statutes; we have indicated what is the real state of the case.

However that may be, its members are all (or nearly all) workingmen; they represent the different nations which form the association.

"The members of the bureau," says M. Testut,

"are taken from itself; there is a president, a general secretary, a treasurer, and as many special secretaries as there are different countries, which are found in the sections of the International.

"These last are for correspondence with the special secretaries designated by each section; they are the attornies who alone receive, in their respective cities, the communications made by the general council, give shares to the members, receive the assessments which they transmit to London, keep the general council acquainted with the movement of the working class, address to it the reports upon the situation of each section, upon its needs, its aspirations, and initiating it into all that is said and done in their center of action; but for making these communications, there are hierarchic rules to be observed; they can not immediately address the president of the general council. All their correspondence must be sent to the particular secretary, who represents before the council the nation to which they belong. Thus the secretaries of Rouen, Lyons, Paris, Marseilles, can and must correspond only with the citizen Eugène Dupont. It remains to be added, that in the countries where the restrictive laws prevent the formation of a center of action with safety, the mission of the general council is to correspond with the individual branches; such was the situation of France before 1869."

The general council plays the rôle of executive power in the International, and as such it is permanent.

The legislative power, that the force of circumstances obliges to unite once a year and in an extremely short session, is the congress.

It is to the general council that belongs the care of organizing the congress, of determining upon the definite programme, of sending it, by means of correspondents, to all the federations and sections. This programme is, moreover, published in advance by all the journals which the association rules.

If the general council organizes the congress, it does not convoke it, at least in ordinary circumstances.

Each congress indicates, before separating, the place and time of the next congress. At the fixed epoch, and without which there would be need of a special convocation, all the delegates assemble at the appointed day and place. The general council has the right, in case of urgent business, to urge this reunion before the epoch indicated; it can, also, if an unforeseen circumstance renders such a measure necessary, change the place named for the rendezvous. But it cannot, in any case, put off the time. Such is, at least, the letter of the law. The events of the last year have already constrained the members of the association to suffer for once the violation, and a note which we find in one of the organs of the association, *L'Egalité* [issue of September 3rd, 1870,] tells us that it is the general council itself which "has decided to adjourn the convocation of the general congress to a time more favorable for the reunion of the delegates of the workingmen of all countries." It is lawful to inquire if the general council would not find itself this year in the face of a moral impossibility, at least as evident as was in 1870 the material impossibility. But if it is otherwise, it will be very interesting to know the *public report* that the executive power should address to the congress, and the "picture of the progress of the association," which it is under obligation to present to it. We are curious to know if the burning of our buildings and our private houses, as well as the massacre of a part of the clergy of Paris, of two generals, of a republican journalist, and of thirty or forty *gendarmes*, will be glorified as a title of honor for the association which has given birth to the central committee of the national guard and to the *Commune* of Paris.

IV. PARTICULAR STATUTES OF THE FEDERATIONS.

We find at the close of the volume the statutes of the association as they were adopted at the first congress, held at Geneva in 1866. The principal laws are to be found in what we have said of the general organization of the society.

The different federations can also have their particular laws, with the sole condition that they contain nothing contrary to the general laws adopted by the whole society. Most of the federations exercise this right. M. Testut has published a certain number of these particular statutes. They ordinarily present nothing very curious; they almost all offer laws differing very little from one another, and all inspired by the same spirit.

Those of the Paris federation have this singularity, that, by a coincidence wholly fortuitous, they bore a date which was to receive, a year later, a sad celebrity ; it was the 18th of March, 1870, that the text of the plan which contained them was definitely determined upon at a reunion at which, among other personages destined to play a rôle that year, were present Malon, Combault, and Avrial. A month later, the 19th of April, they were discussed and accepted at a general reunion of the Paris section, presided over by Varlin.

We find here, in every line, the trace of that incurable defiance which is the vice of democracy generally, but especially of the democracy of Paris. We remember with what ardor the orators of the electoral reunions of 1869, and the writers of socialistic tracts insisted that the candidates designated by the party should pledge themselves in writing to tender their resignation at the first summons of their electors. This novelty, which they could not introduce into the laws of the country, has at least found place in the statutes of the federation of Paris : "Each section nominates and changes its delegates when it pleases." (Article 2d.) "At the first meetings of April and October, the federal council will nominate its bureau. The members of the bureau are constantly liable to be recalled by the council."

Without doubt, the skill of the managers in maintaining themselves always in the places which they had assigned to themselves at the beginning of the work, lessens the practical inconveniences which perpetual changes in the officials of the association would present. But, on the other hand, in order to guard their positions, the leaders are obliged to submit, in many cases, to the influence of the masses whom they hope to lead. This, probably, is the explanation of some of the most enormous mistakes committed either before, or especially after March 18th, 1871, by those among them who were represented as the most intelligent. The demagogic party has always been, of all parties, the one in which the head is most often led by the tail. Everyone knows the celebrated saying, "I must follow them, since I am their leader." The leaders of the International had abundant occasion to borrow this from the ancient idol of the Jacobin party.

In the statutes of the Lyons federation, we notice only one detail, instructive, despite its childishness; article 7, after having regulated the departments of the federal committee, adds: "The committee has no president, but a special secretary and treasurer."

It is not to be believed that this abolition of the presidency was inscribed there by chance. No, this not very formidable title of president of a committee, suffices to excite the jealousy, always on the alert, of the socialistic party. The question of the presidency had been gravely proposed and discussed in 1869 at the congress of Basle which voted, with the utmost seriousness, the following resolution:

"Considering that it is not becoming for a workingmen's society to maintain in its bosom a monarchial and authoritative principle by admitting presidents, even when they are not invested with any power, distinctions purely honorary being yet an injury to democratic principles;

"The congress enjoins upon all the sections and workingmen's societies affiliated with the International to abolish the presidency in their constitution." This recommendation was promptly followed by nearly all.

It is thus that we see Varlin, November 21st, in the "committee of initiative of the syndical chamber of bakers," at which he was present in the capacity of member of the International, carrying through "the democratic principle of the election of the president at each assembly," by saying that "it is an act of liberty, equality, and fraternity." The official report of the meeting mentions that "the unanimous assent proves to Varlin that he is understood."

We see, from these facts, with what sentiment the decree of the Commune proceeded, which abolished the title of general as hardly democratic; we see why the Commune had at each meeting one or two new presidents; we understand, finally, why all the great men of the 18th of March, who seized upon the different offices, were contented with the modest title of delegates. How could the conspirators of the central committee bear to see these brilliant titles of general and minister, attached to the names of comrades with whom they had touched glasses in the drinking shops of

Montmartre, they who could not even bear the modest title of president of a workingmen's committee?

V. BUDGET OF THE INTERNATIONAL. — GENERAL AND PARTICULAR BUDGETS. — YEARLY AND MONTHY ASSESSMENTS. — "LA CAISSE DU SOU."

It remains for us, in exhausting the details of the organization of the International, to explain the budget of the association. It is not necessary to say, that the official accounts deceive us, and that the documents, which would permit us to estimate, even approximately, the receipts and expenses of this army of the demagogy, are not in our hands.

That which we can say is, that according to the terms of the statutes, every member of the association must, at first, at the time of his admission, pay a right of entrance of 50 *centimes*, in exchange for which he receives his ticket of membership. This ticket is afterwards gratuitously renewed each year.

He is bound, besides, to pay an infinitely small assessment of 10 *centimes* a year, designed to meet the general expenses of the society. The funds arising from this source are remitted to the general council, which has the management of them.

Moreover, each federation demands from its members a special assessment for the expenses of the federation itself. At Lyons and at Paris, this assessment is fixed at 10 *centimes* apiece monthly. The Lyons federation is charged to pay upon this sum, the annual assessment of its members for general funds: it seems that it is not the same at Paris. However that may be, the sum payable annually by each associate is sufficiently light: 1 *franc*, 20 *centimes* at Lyons, 1 *franc*, 30 *centimes* at Paris, that is not paying too dear for the honor of belonging to a society which aspires to govern the world and commences by burning it.

One can belong to it at a still better bargain, since the federation of those sections, whose seat is at Geneva, only demands 10 *centimes* a year from each of its members.

It seems, however, that such modest sums did not come in easily, if we judge by the precautions inscribed in the statutes against members or sections who delayed their payments.

In 1859, the Congress of Basle, instructed probably by a mournful experience of the slight alacrity which brothers and friends showed in opening their purses, inscribed in its administrative resolutions article 8, full of meaning:

"In future only those delegates of the societies, sections, or groups affiliated with the International, and who have obeyed the rule of the general council as regards the payment of their assessments, will be admitted to a seat and a vote in the congress."

The statutes of the Paris federation are not less instructive:

"One of the delegates of the sections must deposit at the first assembly of the month, the calculated sum in the hands of the treasurer, and he gives notice at the third monthly reunion, by a note affixed to the room, of the sections which have violated the rule.

"After a month's delay, the suspension of the section is legal; its delegates have no longer voice in the council: after three months it is announced that its name has been struck off."*

We add that the members of the association are without doubt, to pay each to their respective sections an assessment, much larger than that which they pay to their federation, and to the general council. In a letter of Varlin's, dated at Lille, where he went in the month of April, 1870, to organize a section of the International, we find the following lines;

"The isolated adherents deposit 10 *centimes* a week, the members of the sections 5 *eentimes* a week equally. You perceive we have copied a little from your federation, a little from that of Lyons." (Account given of the three trials, p. 58.)

We can estimate upon the whole at 7 or 8 *francs* almost all the different assessments, regular and obligatory, paid to the different treasuries of the International by its associates in the large cities of France.

These resources are not the only ones, nor doubtless the most important of the society; but its other sources of revenue are not fixed, and they are not so easy to be understood by an outsider.

Thus, in the accounts rendered of the different

* The complete text of these statutes can be found in the book of M. Oscar Testut.

suits which have been brought against it, there is, in each instance, question as to the *caisse fédérative du sou** without very well defining the exact meaning of the expression. Following the particular information that we have been able to collect, we have reason to believe that there existed a treasury filled by means of voluntary subscriptions of 5 *centimes* apiece weekly, collected in the workshops and furnished in great part by the workingmen who were not yet personally members of the association, but who proposed to become so, and many of whom even consented to sustain it with their money, without becoming members.

We see also in the statutes of the Paris federation, (article 9) that "the council can with motives of aid, vote for greater expenses in its budget, and fix proportionately the supplementary contribution of each section; but in this case the contribution remains purely optional."

Finally, that which seems to be the most powerful arm of the association, when the question arises of sustaining a strike, to which its leaders attach great importance, is the subscriptions.

A letter from Varlin to Aubry, dated at Paris,

---

* "Write to Theisz for the federal chamber of the workingmen's societies, to Lombard for *la caisse fédérative du sou*, to Langevin for the International." (Letter from Varlin to Aubry, quoted by Theisz at the audience of July 2nd, 1870.)

"The strike of the wool-spinners at Vienna is ended. *La caisse du sou* voted them a loan of 1000 *francs*, of which 500 were sent together." (Letter of Varlin, January 9th, 1869.)

There is mention in several other documents of loans, often important, made to the workingmen on strike by the *caisse du sou.*

January 8th, 1869, and quoted in the indictment at the third trial, will show us sufficiently what abundant resources they were to furnish to the budget of the International:

"When we received your first appeal with the circular, we thought that the strike had not great importance as regards numbers: that the cotton districts could nearly suffice to sustain it and that you demanded our moral aid rather than material. So we content ourselves with opening a subscription in the book-bindery and among the friends with whom we are in daily relation, reserving to ourselves to make appeal to the whole working population of Paris; if the strike should become general, that is to say, if the manifestations put into execution the resolution which you describe in your circular.

"You should understand that the subscription is a means to be used, but not abused, because then it would be exhausted. Now, at Paris, we have almost continually subscriptions on hand in each profession, either for a comrade injured by an accident, or to sustain a strike in a similar profession or with which it is found in almost permanent contact, and a strike must take proportions large enough in order to make a general appeal with any chance of being heard: for example, the strike of the workers in bronze, which numbered from three to four thousand workmen, the strike at Geneva which comprised ten professions at once.

"If the strike of the workmen should acquire greater extension, you can count upon our making heroic efforts to sustain them. But until then, we have thought best to circulate our subscription among ourselves and without noise."

We find there not only the exposé of the theory, but the most interesting details of the practice of the subscriptions at Paris. This practice would evidently vary infinitely according to more or less generosity, greater or less ability of the workmen of each country, of each city: but it varies also according to the usages and the rules of each federation, as is also proved by the correspondence seized at Varlin's house, when the third suits were directed against the association.

Most of our readers doubtless remember the strike of the builders which broke out in Geneva in the spring of 1868. The central committee of Geneva made haste to write to all the federations to demand instantly subsidies. The affair was urgent; it was considered of extreme importance that it should not undergo, in the first great effort that the association made in Switzerland, a check which would bring discredit upon it in that country. One of the secretaries, Jules Paillard, distinctly declared to Varlin:

"Here we are in the face of three thousand workingmen without work, whose greatest crime, in the eyes of these gentlemen, is that they belong to the International Association, which they have sworn to destroy, being a foreign society, receiving orders from London, Paris, Brussels, and who declare that they will do their utmost to hinder unanimity among the workingmen. The question is of the gravest character: it concerns the triumph of the association in our country or its destruction. This is why the central committee make an urgent appeal to the general council of London, to advise all the sections of England, France, Belgium, and Germany to come to the aid of their brothers in Geneva. The success of the cause depends upon prompt and decisive action."

A delegate from Geneva, named Graglia, charged to go to London to solicit aid from the English branch, wrote in despair to Varlin, April 7th, "The English societies are veritable fortresses, and I very much fear that we shall not raise a sum large enough to help our compatriots, this week. Without doubt, I am the first to acknowledge it, in some weeks these same societies will furnish us sums beyond our actual needs; but as I have made several of these gentlemen understand, it is immediate help that we must have. But what can you do? the laws forbid them in a positive manner. We must submit."

While the English workingmen, as formal as the members of Parliament, let the question of aid to be accorded to strikers pass through all the regulated forms, the French Internationals put their hands in their pockets without so much formality. On the 5th of April, Varlin, in the name of the Paris committee, published in *L'Opinion nationale* that a subscription, designed to sustain the strike at Geneva, was opened in the bureaus of the association. It made an appeal to the workingmen of every profession; the lists circulated everywhere, and in fifteen days the workingmen of Paris, not only the builders, but the lithographers, the printers, and the tinmen, remitted to the Paris committee sums which amounted to more than 10,000 *francs.*

Accordingly, April 9th, Graglia wrote to Varlin: "I have just received your letter, which has given me great pleasure, for it assures me once more that the sentiment of solidarity is not a vain word in the working population of Paris. Ah! my friend, if we men of the French language have frivolity of character, nevertheless we cannot remain insensible and cold before a necessity like that which presents itself at this time, while London, that immense city, with its million workingmen, with its formidable societies, with its *trade-unions*,—very well! with all that, with all those advantages which in our hands would accomplish such wonders, it lets a society perish to which itself gave birth, and that because of its selfish rules; for, up to this time, a sum of 500 *francs* only has been voted; the other societies have told us to wait.

"Without doubt the remedy will come when the malady will have ceased to exist; but in the eyes of the English, the rules will have been scrupulously respected, and that suffices for them."

What may be, on the average, the amount of the sums furnished by all these assessments, obligatory as well as optional? It is absolutely impossible for us to estimate it, even approximately. Only it is certain that these sums, in every case very considerable, the great number of members of the society being considered, are always insufficient on account of the immense needs caused by the strikes which occur at every moment.

Everyone has read in the journals of the International the beautiful sentences which the leaders of the society write for their readers, upon the misfortunes of the proletaries, reduced by the exigencies of infamous capital to leave their work and desert the workshops where others profit by their misery.

A private letter from Varlin, quoted at the audience of June 22nd, 1870, in the speech of the imperial advocate, shows that these distinguished citizens speak with less emotion of these sufferings when they have no hearers :

" I tell you nothing of the strike of the leather-dressers, which we declared finished ten days ago, and which leaves us four hundred men without work, to whom we cannot even give bread. Day before yesterday, they wished to sack their former workshops and chase the *mogs* who have replaced them. Happily they were restrained, but *we are very much annoyed by this affair.* The strikers have gone to find Rochefort at the *Corps Législatif,* no longer knowing to whom to commend themselves ; they have sent to the bureau of *La Marseillaise,* where 200 *francs* have been given them, which the hungriest shared upon the *placc des Victoires.*"

Go, brave misguided workingmen, leave at the first command of your leaders, the workshop where you gain the bread for your family by honest labor. When the subscriptions which your comrades have furnished shall be exhausted, when your wives beg you with tears for your starving children a piece of bread which you cannot give them, the journalists, whose fortune you are making, may, perhaps, throw you by their servants a meagre charity, but take care not to trouble with your complaints the chiefs who have commanded you to leave off work. You might *annoy* the citizen Varlin!

CHAPTER VI.

THE CONGRESSES.

I. DATES OF THE CONGRESSES.—NAMES OF THE DELEGATES WHO TOOK PART IN THEM.

We have already stated that the founders of the International had resolved in 1864 to hold, the following year, at Brussels, the first general assembly of the society, which would give an actual existence to it by sanctioning the provisional statutes drawn up in London. It is well known that this project could not be put into execution, and that it was necessary to delay a year the convocation of the first congress.

It was opened in Geneva, September 3d, 1866, in the hall of the Treiber brewery, Jung, member and delegate of the general council of London, presiding. The total number of the delegates amounted to sixty.

Paris was represented by Murat, Varlin, Bourdon, Tolain, Guillard, Malon, Perrachon, Camélinat, Cultin, Chemalé, and Fribourg; Rouen by Aubry; and Lyons by Schettel, Richard, Secretan, and Bondy.

The second congress was held at Lausanne in 1867. It was opened September 2d, in the grand hall of the Casino, under the presidency of Eugène Dupont, secretary of the French branch of the general council of London.

The Section of Paris was represented there by Marly, Fribourg, Garbe, Pioley, Reymond, Chemalé, Murat, Tolain, and de Beaumont; those of Caen and Condé-sur-Noireau, by Charles Longuet, journalist; that of Rouen by Aubry. The other French sections which sent delegates were those of Lyons, Neuville (Rhône), Villefranche (idem), Bordeaux, and Marseilles.

There were in all, for all the countries of Europe represented at this reunion, seventy-one delegates.

They numbered nearly a hundred the next year at Brussels, where the third congress met. It was opened September 6th, under the presidency of Jung, of London, in the hall of the national theater *du Cirque.* The last meeting took place on the 13th. Among the names of the delegates we notice those of MM. Tolain, Murat, Theisz, Roussel, Pindy, Flahaut, and Henry. The latter is designated as a mechanic, president of the Workingmen's Committee of the Exposition and sent by the association of faucet-makers. His surname is not given. We do not know whether he was one of the numerous Henrys who under different titles had important commands in the army of the Commune.

The fourth congress was held at Basle, in 1869. It was opened on Monday, September 6th. Eighty delegates were present. Even America took part in it; Mr. Cameron, sent by the National Labor Union of the United States and of the workingmen's congress of Philadelphia represented there, it is said, eight hundred thousand laborers of the new world.

It is probable enough that, among all these laborers from beyond the sea, there were some thousands and even some hundreds of thousands who were profoundly ignorant of the existence of their representatives and the commission which he professed to have received from them.

Among the representatives of the French sections we will mention Aubry, of Rouen, Varlin, Roussel, Flahaut, Dereure, Albert Richard, without forgetting the inevitable Murat, Pindy, Chemalé and Tolain. A journalist, to-day deputy of Paris, M. Langlois, figured there as delegate of the syndical chamber of the metal-turners of Paris. The oval-makers of Lyons, who had just made themselves notorious because of their strike, sent a Russian Communist, M. Bakounine, publicist.

Before separating, the delegates had named the first Monday of September 1870, for their next reunion. Paris was unanimously chosen as the place of rendezvous. The suits instituted in France against the International in the first months of 1870, would have already inspired the general council with the idea of choosing another city for the convocation of the congress, when the declaration of war, and the events which followed rendered all reunion impossible in whatever place it might be.

None of these four congresses were the cause or occasion of political complications of real importance. We will speak in another chapter of the conferences which took place in the train of the the first, between the French delegates and a minister of Napoleon III, who had not yet renounced the idea of gaining the International to the cause of the Empire.

For the present we will only occupy ourselves with the problems discussed in these four congresses, and the solutions which they received there.

A "French positivist" published in London, during the actual reign of the Commune, interesting political notes on the present situation in France. He recapitulated in a very exact and faithful manner the theories of the International, which were, we know, those of the large majority of the members of the so-called Communal Assembly installed at the *Hôtel de ville;* "Their philosophy," he said, "is atheism, materialism, negation of all religion; their political programme is summed up in absolute individual liberty, obtained by the suppression of all government, and the division of nationalities into communes more or less federated. Their political economy consists essentially in the dispossession, with compensation, of the capitalists and the appropriation of their money, instruments of labor and land, to the workingmen's associations. Their historic theory is that the nobility and the *bourgeoisie* have had their time and that of the proletarian has come. They exclude from the society all those who are outside of the laboring classes."

The author of these notes adds that if the members of the Commune did not publish this programme, it was because they felt that their doctrines were "too strong even for the revolutionary party," and that "they preferred to defer imposing them, until the triumph of the insurrection."

All the ideas exposed by the editor of these political notes, are actually those of the International, and are found developed in the reports, discourses, and resolutions of the congresses in the grand reinforcement of neologisms and of abstract formulas which show some pretensions to Science.

Their journals, particularly those which were published in Belgium and Switzerland, reproduced them equally in every number for several years, but freeing them generally from the pretentious dress with which the pedantry of the fathers of the demagogic church had surrounded them, and often putting them in the most violent and gross forms.

But these doctrines are not found from the first, developed in all their ugliness and brutality in the heart of that part of the working classes which belonged to the International. Time was necessary in order that the pure doctrine of popular Communism should become disengaged from all the formulas diffused in the different working groups in quest of one policy, one philosophy, and one political economy.

Moreover, it is a natural law of all assemblies and societies, that no idea, no passion can remain always equal to itself, without decreasing or increasing. In every group of men not long united by a common bond, a certain force is released, a certain movement is manifested, which ordinarily accelerates: wittingly or unwittingly, each of these organized corps, assemblies, or associations, is put on the march in a certain sense and cannot stop itself in the course upon which it has entered.

Sometimes the movement is good and praiseworthy, and there are then the bad who become better by contact with the good, the stupid whose minds open in a society more intelligent than that in which they have at first lived, the violent who become calm, the fools who grow wise; at other times, it is on the contrary, the crowd of rascals, fools, and egotists which carries away the rest; then the sensible men are discouraged, and lose little by little their good sense; the honest men lose each day a little more of their simple honesty; the men who came with minds clear and penetrating give themselves up more and more to phrases, to rhetorical declamations, and end by becoming incapable of distinguishing the true from the false; they let themselves go slowly, at first, down a disastrous descent; the motion soon increases, and they are rolled into the abyss.

The International has not escaped from this law; if we examine the course which it has run four or five years in the path of error and crime, we become frightened.

Only three years elapsed between the first congress, that of Geneva, and the last, that of Basle. The difference between the ideas which dominated in the first and those which triumphed in the last, would lead us to suppose that there must have been long years to have demoralized to such an extent so numerous a mass.

II. THE CONGRESS OF GENEVA AND THE CONGRESS OF LAUSANNE (1866, 1867). — FIRST ATTACKS AGAINST THE PRINCIPLE OF PROPERTY.

In the first months of 1866, the general council of London addressed to all the sections a programme of the questions which their delegates would be invited to consider at the congress of Geneva.

The historic interest which is attached to this document, induces us to reproduce it here literally. Here it is as we find it in one of the official publications of the International:

"1st. Organization of the International Association; its ends; its means of action.

"2d. Workingmen's societies,—their past, their present, their future; stoppage; strikes,—means of remedying them; primary and professional instruction.

"3d. Work of women and children in factories, from a moral and sanitary point of view.

"4th. Reduction of working hours, — its end, bearing, moral consequences; *obligation of labor for all.*

"5th. Association,—its principle, its applications; cöoperation as distinguished from association proper.

"6th. *Relations of capital and labor;* foreign competition; treaties of commerce.

"7th. Direct and indirect taxes.

"8th. International institutions; mutual credit,

paper money, weights, measures, coin, and language.

"9th. Necessity of abolishing the Russian influence in Europe by the application of the principle of the right of the people to arrange for themselves, and the reconstitution of Poland upon democratic and social bases.

"10th. *Standing armies* in their relations with production.

"11th. Religious ideas,—their influence upon the social, political, and intellectual movement.

"12th. Establishment of a society for mutual help; aid, moral and material, given to the orphans of the association."

We are far from presenting this programme as excellent in itself, and still farther from approving all the solutions given to the problems which it proposed, particularly to those whose terms we have italicized. It should be, however, remarked that the question of property, which was to take such a prominent place in the other congresses, was not even proposed in the first, at least in a direct manner.

Besides, as for the question of religious ideas and their influence upon the social, political, and industrial movement, although the congress ordered the insertion in the official report of different opinions, little edifying, expressed by a certain number of its members on this subject, it refused to express itself in a formal manner against religions, and passed to the order of the day.

They also had the wisdom not to yield to the

enthusiasts who wished to press the congress to strike a blow at "Russian despotism in Europe," and to implore the "reconstitution of Poland upon democratic and social bases."

The French mind, very friendly to generalizations, to syntheses and systems of universal and radical reform, gains a victory over the more practical mind of the English, always fixed upon ends more modest, but possible to attain; the trade-unions were blamed for occupying themselves too exclusively with immediate quarrels, and they were advised to fight "against the capitalist system itself, and to aim at the great end, the emancipation of the working class." That truly was neither good in itself, nor even clever from the point of view at which the members of the congress placed themselves; but good sense had, in part, its revenge in the deliberation upon the cöoperative societies, where some of the most important members of the assembly combatted energetically the idea expressed in advance of directing the cöoperative movement by imposing upon it a single from.

At the Congress of Lausanne, although only one year had elapsed since the Congress of Geneva had passed these comparatively moderate resolutions there was already remarked a change deep and most to be regretted, in the spirit of the decisions adopted. Thus the coöperative societies in whom was acknowledged, in 1866, the right of developing themselves at will, were signalized, in 1867, as "tending to constitute a fourth state having below it a fifth state still more miserable." In other words the sentiment which prevails in this question, is a sentiment of jealousy against the associated workingmen, who, thanks to their intelligence, labor and spirit of order, had succeeded in constituting for their society and for each of its members, a capital small or large, which they did not care to give up to comrades less intelligent, less industrious, and less economical. The congress, obedient to an instinct of low envy against those who are guilty of succeeding by their labor, declares "that social transformation can only work in a radical and definite manner by means acting *upon the whole of the society,* and conformable to reciprocity and justice;" nevertheless, it admits that the efforts of workingmen's associations must be encouraged "only to make disappear as much as possible from the heart of these associations, *the predominance of capital over labor,* that is to say, to introduce the idea of mutuality and federation," which plainly signifies only to make to disappear in a given association all difference between those who have already worked a long time and to good purpose, and those who are only beginning to put themselves to work, only to divide among the associations where want of discipline, disorder and idleness rule, the benefits acquired by those who submit themselves to rule, who labor and economize.*

---

* The congress of the Belgian sections of the International which met at Brussels, in May, 1869, retnrns to this question of coöperative societies. We extract from the summary account published by *L'Internationale,* (May 30th, 1869,) the following passage:

Communism which had not entered into the first congress or at least had not dared to speak, has already a peremptory tone in the second. At Lausanne in fact, after having implored federation between the associations, that is to say, the abandonment to the profit of the idle and incapable of that which the industrious and skilful workingmen had gained, it demands that one should give to the "State proprietor the means of transport and circulation, in order to abolish the powerful monopoly of the large companies, which in submitting the working classes to their arbitrary laws, attack both the dignity of man and individual liberty."

However, it only dared to declare war to the workingmen's societies and the large companies; it had up to this time only claimed property in ap-

---

Hermans. "We wish societies of production other than those which we see founded at Liége; we wish to reach a partial amelioration of the laboring class and not only of a group of fifteen new rivals, new employers. *We wish the society of production to be based upon the societies of resistance; they only ought to be benefited and not the managing workingmen.*" (This idea is approved by several speakers.)

Thus the associated workingmen will give their time, their labor, will pledge their names, all that they possess (we do not forget that the moment that they work in their own name, on their own acconnt, a failure will be to lose everything). If they fail, it is they personally who will be ruined. If they succeed, their money will serve to maintain the voluntary idleness of strikers! We can recall, finally, on the subject, a passage from an interesting article in 1850, in *L'Atelier.* We shall see that at this time those of the associations founded in 1848 which had succeeded, did not care to make, as they were urged, *common cause and treasury* with those which were in danger from the incapacity of the managers or the laziness of the associates. We quoted this article, chap. II, p. 22.

pearance collective. Individual property was respected in the Congresses of 1866 and 1867, or at least they had only to repulse the attacks of the advance-guard, the incursions of some Uhlans of Communism.

At Brussels, in 1868, it underwent a general assault which was opened upon it by all the united forces of the association, without excepting even those who believed in good faith that they were marching to its defense.

In the sitting of the National Assembly of June 16th, 1871, where was voted the nomination of a committee charged with opening an inquiry into the insurrection of March 18th, M. Tolain undertook, we remember, the defense of the International, of which he even proposed to relate to us the whole history, if an entire sitting should be given to this recital. According to him the association passed through two very different periods, one which precedes, the other which follows the first suits directed against the bureau of Paris in 1868. Its principles and its actions had been absolutely irreproachable, until that unfortunate trial, which alone had the sad power of making it "deviate from its line of conduct and of commencement."

The comparison we have just made between the first and second congresses, both anterior to the trials, proves sufficiently that we only see at Brussels the logical development of principles in the germ from the foundation of the association and of passions which had already shown their power at Lausanne after having only been suspected at Geneva.

We do not doubt the sincerity of M. Tolain, but since he did not combat the resolutions voted in 1867, concerning workingmen's societies and the "means of transportation and circulation," and had a fair chance to defend a year later, the principle of individual property, he is, whatever he says and whatever he thinks, among the adversaries of property, which is in reality also completely denied by the *mutualists* and by the *collectivists.*

III. THE CONGRESS OF BRUSSELS (1868).—IT VOTES THE CONFISCATION BY THE STATE OF MINES, QUARRIES, RAILROADS, FORESTS, AND ARABLE LANDS.—M. TOLAIN.

Before entering upon the discussion which, without doubt, was nearest the heart of the majority of its members, the congress of Brussels commenced by examining various other questions.

It recognized the legitimacy and the necessity of strikes in the actual state of war between capital and labor; declared that there was the place "to submit them to certain rules, to conditions of organization and opportunity;" and decided upon the creation of councils of arbitration, charged with superintending the application of these rules. It declared also "that machines, like all other instruments of labor, ought to belong to the laborers themselves and avail to their profit;" and it decided to communicate to all the sections, in order that they might study with great care, a draught of rules "for the creation of a bank of exchange at the cost price."

But the most important of the questions which it considered, that which gave rise to the longest discussions, and in which the foolish ideas, absurd prejudices, and envious passions had the fullest scope, was that of property.

In the sixteenth sitting, Murat read the conclusions adopted in the *administrative sitting*,—that is to say, in secret committee. It is all a theory of property, or rather, a code of universal confiscation.

According to these profound reformers, "the quarries, coal and other mines, as well as the railroads, should belong to the social collectivity, represented by the state, but by the state regenerated," which would give them "not to the capitalists, as at present, but to the workingmen's societies."

The economic evolution (to use the euphemism of of these gentlemen), should make "the admission of arable land to the collective property a social necessity," and "the land should be given to agricultural companies, as the mines to mining companies, the railroads to workingmen's companies."

Finally, the canals, roads, telegraphic lines, and forests, should "remain as the collective property of the society."

These radical measures are accompanied by a mass of considerations, in which absurdity and violence seek to hide themselves as well as they can behind a vast array of grand words, apparently scientific.

Would it not be more simple to spare themselves the trouble of collecting all these fine terms of *economic evolution, social collectivity, scientific and rational farming*, and to acknowledge simply that they wished to take all the good things of this world for the simple reason that they wanted them, that they thought themselves strong enough to secure them? This would be shorter and more frank

Of the forty-nine delegates present at the time of voting on these fine conclusions, thirty voted for their adoption, only four opposed them, and fifteen abstained from voting.

M. Tolain explained this abstaining by reading the following declaration:

"Considering that, according to us, the question of property was only made the order of the day at the last sitting; that it has only been studied from a general point of view, in an altogether insignificant manner; from an agricultural point of view in an incomplete manner; that in view of the affirmation of a certain number of delegates, who say they are not informed on the subject, it was natural to defer the question to the next congress;

"The delegates whose names follow, who have abstained and who have voted against it, decline thus the responsibility of the vote." (The signatures follow.)

It is upon this declaration that M. Tolain strengthened himself to say, March 16th, at the National Assembly that "the founders of the International, in their programme, in the memorial which they published, had from a social point of view, defended individual property."

We do not doubt the perfect good faith of M.

Tolain. We doubt it so much the less, as, in the official account rendered of the 14th sitting of the congress of Brussels, we read a discourse in which the citizen Coenen, of Antwerp, is astonished "that certain members of the International rise up so strongly against Communism," and declares that "associate Tolain is in error when he regards individual property in the soil as a condition of individual liberty."

But if M. Tolain is authorized in imagining that he was a veritable defender of property at Brussels, one of his opponents in the same congress, the Belgian Communist De Paepe, was evidently truthful and logical when he replied :

"We only endeavor to extend to agricultural property that which M. Tolain and the other enemies of the collective property of land, admit to be very good for mines, railroads, roads, canals, etc. ; there are no absolute partizans of individual property here ; we are all more or less Communists, if so be that the considerations of the committee can be regarded as Communism. In fact, we do not ask that the state should become farmer or hire working farmers, any more than they ask that the state should become miner and hire miners, but we wish that the land should be conceded to large farming companies, as the mines, railroads, etc., to large working companies. Why deal differently with the mine, or the field below ground, and the field properly so-called, which is only a mine on the surface of the earth, a mine from which are extracted vegetables in place of stones, marble, minerals, and coal? We believe ourselves more logical than our opponents; the land, as what is beneath the land, being both given gratuitously to humanity by nature, we claim property in it for all humanity, and we demand the farming of it by the associations."

It is incontestable that M. de Paepe and the Communists have logic on their side of the discussion with the Mutualists; but do we still wish to see what securities the opinions defended by M. Tolain offer to the society, and to judge if he has the right to call himself the defender of individual property?

We have only to open the report rendered of the Congress of Basle, published by M. Mollin, "delegate of the Paris circle of proletarian positivists."

IV. CONGRESS OF BASLE (1869).—ABOLITION OF PROPERTY.—M. TOLAIN AGAIN.—MUTUALISTS AND COLLECTIVISTS.—DISCUSSION UPON THE RIGHT OF INHERITANCE.—SOCIAL ADJUSTMENT.

In a sitting of the Congress of Basle, a delegate, named Robin, asserted in a speech in favor of *Collectivism*, that is to say of *Communism*, that the peasants are not at all hostile as the *Individualists* suppose; immediately, M. Tolain, who marked this last term, hastened to declare "that he regarded this distinction as an injury and a calumny, and said that he and his friends were *Mutualists*."*

Now, without taking the trouble to ascertain the

* Report of the Congress of Basle, by G. Mollin, p. 20.

exact meaning of this new word *Mutualist*, which reappears so often for some months in the discussions between socialists, we find even in the report of M. Mollin, the system proposed by this school the pretended friend of individual property.

It was M. Tolain in person who, Friday, September 10th, proposed to the Congress of Basle to declare that "in order to realize the emancipation of laborers," it was necessary to transform the leases, rents, salaries, in a word, all the contracts of rent into contracts of sale; that then property being continually in circulation would cease to be abusive by this very fact.

Now the preceding discussions sufficiently show what the mutualist school means by the transformations of contracts of rent into contracts of sale. It is simply an application of the theory dear to the whole International, which condemns the interest on capital. According to the system of M. Tolain and his friends, all interest or rent payed for a sum of money due, or for a house or land taken on hire, should be applied to the reduction of the capital to be reimbursed, or of the payment of the real estate occupied. So that, if I had borrowed 1000 *francs*, and I pay each year 50 *francs* to my creditor, at the end of twenty years, I should have reimbursed him, and he would have nothing more to claim from me; if I occupy a house worth 100,000 *francs*, and I pay each year 5,000 *francs* to the proprietor, at the end of five years I should have acquired a quarter of this real estate, half at the end of ten years, and the whole in twenty years, and I should have become sole and legitimate proprietor.

Such is the theory spread through the world, especially by P.-J. Proudhon, inventor of the celebrated formula : *property is robbery*, and adopted by the honorable deputy from Paris who naively considers himself a defender of property.

Consider for a moment whether he was its enemy !

Let us add that M. Tolain affirmed that his ideas, so favorable, according to him, to individual property, were shared by an " immense majority of the workingmen of Paris," and that " at *Rouen* equally, in other cities, everywhere, they adhered to this memorial which defended individual property and the transmission of heritage, and which acknowledged the family as the end of Society."

We are sure that M. Tolain did not seek to abuse the good faith of his colleagues of the Assembly, but we ought to state either that he deceived himself or that the ideas of the workingmen of Rouen, which were already little encouraging in 1868, if they were those of the Mutualists, were very like in 1869 those of the Collectivists, since that year, at the Congress of Basle, M. Aubry, who since the foundation of the International was by right of conquest or of birth the accredited and official representative of the workingmen of the capital of the Lower Seine, demanded that " landed property should become collective and be regulated by the communes organized federatively." He had moreover taken great care to place in the conclusions which he had read in congress, a paragraph declaring that it was not he personally, but " the circle of of economic studies of the *arrondissement* of Rouen, composed of all the workingmen's corporations of said *arrondissement*," which considered the property of the soil "only from a collective point of view."

We see what the assertions of M. Tolain are worth when he seeks to encourage us concerning the ideas and tendencies of the society of which he was one of the founders.

Thus, in fact, the unanimity of the Congress of Basle was attained by the suppression of property such as had always existed in every civilized nation, and the delegates all agreeing to condemn these unfortunate proprietors, were divided only upon the question of whether they must be eaten with mutualist or collectivist sauce.

The mines, quarries, railroads, lands, forests, houses, manufactories, machines, and tools of labor, once confiscated under one or other of these two rival forms, and capital, to which besides was not left any means of its creation, condemned to return no interest in any form, it seems that the question of inheritance has no longer a very great practical utility, as was remarked, with reason, by a French delegate, M. Chemalé.

However, the Congress of Basle saw fit to lose several hours in discussing it.

M. Eccarius was of the opinion that in waiting for the realization of collective property, which will solve the question of inheritance, it would "be necessary to adopt transient measures consisting in claiming a considerable rise in the taxes on succession and the application of the larger amount of the tax thus produced, to social ameliorations."

More pressed at the end, the committee demanded of the congress to recognize that "the right of inheritance should be completely and radically abolished, and that this abolition is one of the indispensable conditions of the enfranchisement of labor."

A Belgian, whom the *bourgeoisie* of Brussels, without doubt, little cared to see at the head of a provisional government if Belgium should ever sustain a revolution, M. de Paepe, was of the opinion that "inheritance in a direct line, freed from its abuses, is an excellent element of progress for humanity, and should be maintained as encouraging economy and family feeling;" but he did not believe in the efficacy of the abolition of inheritance in the adjustment of society. He no longer expected "amicable adjustment in accordance with the sentiments which the *bourgeois* society professed in respect to the workingmen."

Finally, the delegate of the oval-makers of Lyons, Bakounine, the Russian *nihilist,* expressed himself clearly against the right of inheritance: "He is willing," says M. Mollin, "that the clothes of the parents be transmitted to the children, but that is all."

It appears that this *all* did not seem sufficient to those delegates who had children, and some other trifles than a blouse to leave them, for against thirty-two voices which spoke in favor of the abolition of inheritance, there were twenty-three voices which demanded its maintenance, and seventeen delegates who were silent, not daring, doubtless, either to vote resolutions absolutely contrary to sentiments the most deeply rooted in the human heart, nor to unite with the *bourgeois* reaction in opposing them.

An amendment proposed by the tailor Eccarius, born member of the general council, which consisted in limiting on one side the right of making wills, and increasing on the other side the taxes on succession in direct inheritance, was immediately rejected by a very large majority ; thus, no conclusion was given to this discussion.

We have met in the résumé of the speech of M. de Paepe, with an expression which had already, for one or two years, made much noise in the Red clubs of Paris, *social adjustment.*

The chief of the Belgian Communists was not the only one who used it, and Bakounine employed it also on his side, in giving this comment, which we advise our readers to read with care : " I understand by social adjustment, the expropriation by law of all actual proprietors, by the abolition of the political and juridical state, which is the sanction and the only guaranty of actual property and of everything that is called juridical law ; and the expropriation, in fact, everywhere and as far as possible, and as soon as possible, by the very force of events and circumstances."

This is what was thought, what was said in 1869 at Basle, only three years after the congress of Geneva. Our readers have been able to follow the gradation of ideas and of language, and see with what rapidity the wave of malignant passions and the level of general madness rose in the International. What would these men have said, if they had been able, according to their first plan, to unite at Paris in 1870?

It is easy to imagine, for, if the congress did not take place, the programme at least was published,* and the manner in which the questions were proposed suffices to show in what sense they would have been solved:

The first was thus conceived: *The necessity of abolishing the public debt. Discussion upon the right of according indemnity.*

The third was relative to the *practical means of converting landed property into social property.*

The fifth treated of the *conditions of coöperative production upon a national scale.*

Finally, the Belgian general council proposed in its own name, as an addtional question, the search for *practical means* to be employed in order to *constitute agricultural sections in the heart of the International.*

Thus: Abolition of the public debt, the most prompt confiscation possible of territorial property, suppression of the workingmen's societies which had succeeded in developing themselves and prospering, thanks to their energy and spirit of order, and in the meantime, active proselyting in order to immediately diffuse through the country the gangrene with which the cities were already infected.

---

* Especially in *L'Égalité* of August 6th, 1870.

These are the resolutions which would have certainly been adopted by the congress of 1870, if events had not rendered reunion impossible.

Let us add, moreover, that this congress was in reality only delayed some months. It was originally to have met at Paris, in September, 1870. It was opened there in March, 1871, at the *Hôtel de ville,* taking this time the name of the Commune of Paris. It deliberated during the last days of March, all of April, and the first twenty days of May.

It put, as well as it could, these theories in practice from the 23d to the 28th of May, and it consoled itself for not being able to confiscate all the houses of Paris, by destroying a great number of them.

CHAPTER VII.

JOURNALS OF THE INTERNATIONAL.

THEIR NUMBER.—HOW THEY SPEAK OF THE BOURGEOISIE, THE ARMY, THE MAGISTRACY, AND THE CLERGY.

We have said that the doctrines sustained in the congresses, most of the time, by the speakers and reporters who have great scientific pretensions and pedantic manners, were afterwards reproduced, developed and commented upon, all through the year by the organs of the association, in a style more accessible to the uninitiated.

M. Testut gives a list of twenty-nine journals which serve as organs to the International on the European continent.

Seven of these sheets are written in French, but none are printed in France; all are published either in Belgium or Switzerland; one of those which appeared in Geneva, *La Cause du Peuple*, although written in French, is the organ of the Russian section of the International.

The others are:

La Réforme sociale, printed in Brussels, but edited by Aubry of Rouen, and written especially in view of the Normandy Socialists.

L'Internationale, which appeared every Saturday at Brussels, since January 16th, 1869.

Le Devoir, organ of the Section of Liège, issued every Sunday.

Le Mirabeau, organ of the Sections of the Valley of the Vesdre, issued every Sunday at Verviers.

L'Egalité, journal of the International Association of Workingmen of Switzerland, issued at Geneva on Saturdays, since January 3rd, 1869. It succeeded to *La Voix de l'avenir*. It was, during the first three months of its existence, the official organ of the Sections of Switzerland. For more than a year it has only appeared at long and very irregular intervals.

La Solidarité, organ of the Sections of the Swiss Federation of the International Association, published at Neuchatel since April 11th, 1870.

The association possesses only one journal in Italy, it is *La Fratellanza* (The Fraternity), organ of the Naples Section. It appears since June, 1869.

It possesses, on the contrary, six which are edited in Spain. Two of them come out in Catalogne: another is published at Palma (Balearic Isles), the other three are printed at Madrid.

All the rest are written in Flemish, Dutch and German. At New York the association possesses a journal edited in German. We do not know exactly how many it has in England, nor even whether it has in Great Britain journals which entirely belong to it.

In France, it has possessed some months *La Marseillaise*, of which it was, as we shall see in another chapter, almost absolute mistress. A great number of demagogic sheets, which appeared in the last days of the Empire or after September 4th, were entirely at its disposal; but we do not believe any of these had been officially recognized as its organ.

Let us see now how those of the sheets which are published in French speak.

In April, 1869, in consequence of a strike which burst out in Seraing, in Belgium, there were produced disorders grave enough to necessitate the intervention of the troops. They were constrained to make use of their arms, and many of the disturbers were struck.

In the number of April 25th, 1869, *L'Internationale* publishes on this subject an article entitled: *A Bourgeois Conspiracy.*

"Formerly," says the author of this article, "there were peoples who conspired against their tyrants. To-day, the case is altered; since the men of the people no longer conspire, but display in broad day-light their plans of proletariat assemblies, their ways and means, their programme and their method, it is the despots which conspire against the people.

"Under whatever political régime we live, republic or monarchial, the despot *par excellence* in actual society, is capital, or to be more explicit, the capitalist class, the *bourgeoisie.* All our rulers, whatever they are, emperors, constitutional kings, presidents of a republic, no longer draw their power, as formerly, from themselves, but from the privileged class, of which they are the representatives, from the capital of which they are the incarnation.

"We have just been present, in Belgium, at one

of these vast conspiracies contrived by the *bourgeois* despots against the popular masses."

The journalist then explains to his readers that the *bourgeoisie,* frightened at the ever growing success of the International, seeks a pretext for suppressing this society which has become too strong. It exerts itself to irritate, by every means, the workingmen whom it wishes to force into a strike, in order to be able to represent this strike as a revolt, to arrest some of the associates and irritate the others.

"No sooner said than done. A manufactory of which persons of high rank were the principal shareholders, gave the signal for the annoyances; strikes, violence, stones thrown at our brave soldiers, firing, massacres, carnage, the abomination of desolation, it is the International which is the cause of all.

"This is the origin of that fearful comedy with tragic acts, which was opened last week and unfolded before our eyes, and of which the proletary soldiers and the proletary workingmen, were the actors, the *bourgeois* the manager, the banks of the Meuse and the plains of Borinage the theatre, but of which the public will not be the dupe.

"What interest do you ask has the International in seeing these mobs? Is it because that it wished that the strikes should succeed and attain their end? But the mob is precisely the means of frustrating them. Is it because that it aims at a revolution, not of form like that of our people in 1830, but of substance, that is to say having for object the abolition of individual landed property, the domination of labor over capital, the abolition of salaries, integral instruction? But mobs only spend in vain an energy and forces which should only be put in play for the great day of social adjustment.

"The *bourgeoisie* alone can have interest in the uprisings of proletaries, because that gives it occasion for crushing its slaves, for terrifying them, for preventing the socialist movement. Now, *ille fecit cui prodest* (he committed the crime who was interested in its commission). By virtue of this principle of law, we demand the arrest of the leaders of our *bourgeoisie*, that is to say of our great manufacturers, of our large speculators and bankers, of our great merchants, of our rich capitalists, of our large landowners, and of their official representatives, and that our companions who have been locked up should be released; it must be that justice, if it is worthy of that august name, shall reach at last the great and only culprits! it must be that the blood of the martyrs of Seraing and of Frameries shall be upon the heads of those whose caused it to flow."

In another article upon the same events, *L'Internationale*, seeking to clear up the "morality of the affair of Seraing," draws this conclusion, among many others:

"The soldier and the *gendarme*, as soon as they have put on their uniform and are loosed, become wild beasts; in consequence, whatever may be the civilization of a country, its liberty will be compromised as long as there is an army. There are no intelligent bayonets. Still less can the intelligence of the officers be counted upon. These unfortunates, brutalized by idleness and the vices which it engenders, are incapable of any honest sentiment. When we disband the army, it will be necessary to subject these gentlemen to a long hygienic and moral treatment before they can be made workingmen.

"In the meantime, we implore fathers of families not to let their children adopt this profession, which leads to debauchery and murder."

M. Testut has taken from different journals of the International passages still more violent, much more odious than those which we have just quoted.

Let us see first how the *bourgeois*, those idlers, who acquire, as everyone knows, their fortune by folding their arms, are treated by the organs of the *workingmen:*

"The *bourgeois* are *afraid;* fear makes them cry out; seeing this formidable power which is organized under their noses and their beards, and *which must swallow them up some day*, they no longer know which way to turn. They see the privileges of capital disappear; may they die a natural death. Amen."—(Extract from the journal *L'Egalité*, January 23d, 1869.)

If they do not decide to hearken to this charitable wish, what future is reserved for them in the republic of the International? It is that which *L'Egalité* of November 27th wishes to teach us:

"When social revolution shall have dispossessed the *bourgeois* of their property for reason of public utility, as they have already dispossessed the nobility and the clergy, what will become of them?

"We cannot answer certainly, but it is probable that the new order of things will give them, according to the expression of one of our friends, a good, infinitely more precious, of labor well paid, at discretion, so that they may no longer be obliged to live by the labor of others, as they have done until now. In case of incapacity for labor on their part, which will be the case with a large number, seeing that they have learned but little how to use their ten fingers, well! well! *we will give them the best of soup.*

"But that is too little, the *bourgeois* will howl.

"Too little, the workingmen will respond, too little! work well paid, at discretion, and soup for the invalids! By Jupiter! you are difficult; we would be very well contented with it in time."

The *bourgeois*, who would be disposed to find *L'Egalité* rather severe for them, will, on the contrary, be pleased with its comparative benevolence when they see what treatment *L'Internationale* (of April 3d, 1870) prepares for them:

"It is related that Tomyris, queen of the Massagetes, attacked by Cyrus, the insatiable warrior, had the misfortune to lose her son in a battle. She swore to avenge him and succeeded in seizing the bandit-conqueror. She had his head cut off, and throwing it into a pailful of water, cried: 'Well, *monster, fill yourself with blood, since you are so fond of it.*'

"Ah! gentlemen *bourgeois*, you shoot the workingmen who dare to rise against their spoilers; you, also, like to pour out blood. *Well: we will thrust your nose into it and will make you lick up even the last drop.*"

The magistracy is not better treated than the *bourgeoisie.* Listen rather to what *L'Internationale* of December 12th, 1869, says of it:

"For a long time it is known by whom it is held concerning the *morality of magistracies, that inviolability no more defends from corruption than a glass cover defends our noses from the odors of cheese. The French magistracy is totally corrupt. The Belgian magistracy is so much advanced* that it marches all alone. *The German magistracy* is equal to its two sisters, and a trio of Eumenides has replaced in these three countries the divine Astrea whom the ancients said ascended into heaven.

"The citizen Bonhorts, of Magdebourg, after twenty-eight days of accusation, has just appeared before that *bundle of scamps called judges.*

The judges are *unmovable and inviolable,* it is true, but in spite of that, they can be, some day, suspended . . . by a rope."

We know enough of the religious principles of the International to guess easily that its journals spare still less, if possible, the clergy, than the *bourgeoisie,* the army, and the magistracy. See how *Le Mirabeau* of Verviers speaks of the priest in the pulpit.

"See the clown who is kicking about in a cask, like the devil in a basin of holy water, insinuating to the amiable flock assembled that his gibberish is pure and sound morality emanating from a supernatural power. This clown with lugubrious manners roars in his cask like thunder, grimaces and contorts himself like an epileptic; he stamps with frenzy, and raises himself like a tragic buffoon, ready to leap close-legged upon his amazed auditors, who hear without frowning the platitudes and wearisome tirades of his tragico-comic repertoire. This kind of charlatan has worn out the seat of his breeches upon the university benches, to chant to us pasquinades in a dead language and to quote to us latinized texts that we do not understand any more than the language of Vidocq, famous user of slang, whom Mercury has in his holy and worthy keeping, if he does not carry him in his bosom. When these buffoons, dressed fantastically, go through the streets bawling like young asses, scenting the hundred *sous* pieces as the hyena scents the putrified flesh, dispatching souls to Charon by different gates, they produce all the effect of maniacs escaped from Bedlam. Such rascals stir one's soul with indignation. All their acts are arbitrary, stamped with perfidy and rascality. They are our very dear brothers in Jesus Christ; we are the Abels of our very dear Cains. Dance, puppets, skipping-jacks, my loves, of your mummeries one is —— forever."

We ask our reader's pardon for having inflicted upon them the reading of these ignoble lines, but it is necessary that honest men should know to what degree of violence and impudence, natures ignorant and coarse can be carried away.

Moreover this frightful abuse, lavished upon all that society is accustomed to respect, does it not explain the crimes which have stupefied Europe and which at first seemed inexplicable?

The journals of the International had for several years excited their readers against the army: the dead bodies of two generals, cowardly assassinated, are proof that they did not preach in the desert.

The journals of the International denounced the corruption and infamy of the magistry: the President Bonjean was slain by their faithful readers.

The journals of the International, not content with teaching under all forms, materialism and atheism, grossly abused the members of the clergy and excited against them the waves of popular hatred. As soon as their disciples were masters of Paris, they pillaged convents and churches: when they saw they were lost, they consoled themselves on their defeat by murdering the archbishop, all the priests, and all the monks whom they had been able to seize.

We see that the editors of these journals wasted neither their time nor their ink.

CHAPTER VIII.

STRIKES.

I. OFFICIAL DOCTRINE OF THE INTERNATIONAL ON THE SUBJECTS OF STRIKES.—PRACTICE DIFFERENT FROM THEORY.—THE STRIKE A POWERFUL MEANS OF PROPAGANDISM.—HOW THE INTERNATIONAL RECRUITED GENERAL DUVAL.

When the International is accused of fomenting strikes, its doctors protest with the greatest energy, bringing forward to the support of their protestations, the finest theories.

Hear Varlin defending himself before the sixth tribunal, May 22nd, 1868: "The International Association does not admit the strike on principle; it believes that it is an anti-economic means. It declared this at Geneva, it declared it everywhere."

All the others accused hold the same language before the tribunal.

The journals of the association speak ordinarily in the same way to their especial public.

In the course of the third trial of the International, at the audience of July 5th, 1870, an accused went still beyond the protestations of the leaders and their journals. With a great supply of learning, quoting M. Levasseur, and Turgot, and Blanqui the economist, threatening to quote Ricardo, Adam Smith and J.-B. Say, he proved that it was the ferocity of the employers which alone drove the workingmen to put themselves on strike. The end of this passage merits being quoted literally:

"That the capitalists, on the occasion of a strike stirred up by their greedy pretensions, are the first to accuse the International of all the evil, I do not find astonishing. They act on this point, like the wolf of the fable who placed himself on the bank of a stream, and accused of troubling his water, the lamb who quenched his thirst below him in the current. The lamb in vain defended himself, claiming that water could not run up hill, all his denials served him nothing; the wolf sought only a favorable occasion for devouring him."

The President: "The lamb, is it the International?"

Answer: "And the wolf is the capitalist."

The accused, who thus compared his comrades and himself to timid lambs, was no other than Frankel, future member of the Commune.

In spite of all these fine declarations, and these touching comparisons, the congress, which did not directly approach the subject of strikes, either at its first or second session, neither at Geneva, nor at Lausanne, considered it at Brussels, and adopted the conclusions read by Brismée in the name of the committee, in which it is said: "that the strike is not a means of completely emancipating the laborer, but that it is often a necessity in the actual state of war between labor and capital; that there is reason for submitting it to certain rules, to some conditions of organization, of opportunity, and of legitimacy;" that consequently there is reason for creating some "societies of resistance" for all the professions which have not yet had them; "afterwards to organize among them societies of resistance of all professions and of all countries, instituting in each local federation of the societies of resistance, *a treasury designed to sustain strikes:* that, in a word, it must *continue in this manner the work undertaken by the International,* and exert itself to make the proletariat enter bodily into this association;" that finally it must constitute in each federation "*a council of arbitration to judge of the opportunity* and the legitimacy of eventual strikes."

Why does the International which speaks out nearly all that it thinks, show itself a long time so reserved upon this point in its declarations?

It is because the strike, which troubles always more or less deeply the public peace and material order, causes at least as much fear to the governments, little friendly to political complications, as to the *bourgeois,* little anxious to see their interests compromised, and that there was no wish, at least in the first years, to alarm too much the governments. It is because, among the workingmen themselves, the strike which condemns to long stoppage, which induces so many privations, so many physical and moral sufferings, is not popular, and that they submit to it,—we speak of the mass and not of the leaders,—only at the last extremity, when they unfortunately deem it to be indispensable. It is because a society which should declare aloud that its end was to organize strikes, would not be much better viewed in the ranks of the workingmen themselves than would be in the ranks of the *bourgeoisie* an association announcing itself as designed to propagate war.

Nevertheless, as much as it is possible to guess the secret thoughts of the founders of the International, their principal end, we might almost say their only end, was at first to establish an understanding between the workingmen of all countries, in order to prevent them from establishing, as had been for a long time customary, competition between them, and to permit them, on the contrary, to impose henceforth by the coalition (or, in the International jargon, by the *solidarization*) of all "*the laborers*" their laws upon employers not associated or *solidarized.*

The idea was simple and practical ; the English mind can be recognized in it, and the details of the organization of the International show sufficiently that it was founded by men who well understood the *trade-unions.* Moreover this project, which took two years to mature, only was put into execution quite seriously, at the banquet of Saint Martin's Hall, in 1864, some months after the vote of the law of coalitions, which rendered strikes legally possible in France. Is it then venturing too far upon the ground of conjecture to suppose that the principal end of the companions of Saint Martin's Hall was to found an association designed to dictate laws to isolated *bourgeois,* by means of formidable strikes which could show that the workingmen of all Europe were well united among themselves ?

But in proportion as success increased and the

French took a more important part in the material and especially intellectual direction of the International, the associates were to conceive more lofty designs. To be content any longer under the dependency on employers, when they believed themselves strong enough to suppress them and reduce them to the *good soup* of charity,* would be altogether too modest. Each day new adherents came by thousands. There were barely some hundreds four or five years ago; already there is united an army of which the soldiers are numbered by hundreds of thousands, by millions. Moreover, it is French, that is to say, great friend of radical revolutions and changes in view; one does not know how to limit one's-self to consider a question as it may be in the commonplaces of the present hour, in the fatiguing and nice details of reality, one adores the grand syntheses, the vast perspectives of an ideal future. Why limit its desires like the English to an increase of some cents upon the daily salary? That word salary, is not even that an insult? Forward, imagination shows the way. Let us forget the cold reality and sketch in broad lines the republic of the future, where there will be neither *bourgeois*, nor hirelings, nor speculators, nor those speculated on, where social harmony will no longer be troubled by the passions, where the most perfect equality will reign, where even the inequalities that nature alone has established, in that moment will find no longer place between the members of the actual society.

---

* See page 132.

To-day this is the dream which dominates in the International. All the associates, those of France, Belgium, and Switzerland, at least, believe firmly in social regeneration, in the early and complete metamorphosis of the old society; but they have made their ideal low and ugly enough so that the English common people can admire it and seek to attain to it. All have but one idea; to bring about the most prompt possible advent of this democratic and social republic, in which all stomachs will be filled at their ease, except those of the *bourgeois.* Now the means of making these fine ideas triumph very quickly, is to draw, in a short time, all the workingmen of the cities and fields into the ranks of the International. Propagandism is the first duty, since that can hasten the advent of the new era.

The strike was at once an end. Little by little experience has proved that it increased in enormous proportions the forces of the association, by persuading strikers to throw themselves into its arms. Then it became a means, but a very precious means. It is Varlin himself who teaches it to us:

"You will tell us if the efforts made by you among the cotton-workers of other houses permit us to arrive at a favorable result. Tell them that they ought to sustain themselves among themselves at once, to the end of meriting the assistance of their brothers in other lands in event of the contest becoming general. Tell them especially *that they ought to be grouped, organized, solidarized, to enter* *into the International league of workingmen, in order to assure themselves of the coöperation of all,* and to be able to guard against all evil contingencies. Is it necessary, moreover, to tell you that? This is what you are doing, and *this strike must be for you a fine occasion for propagandizing.*"*

How the strike brings by hundreds and thousands new adherents to the International, is what one of the accused in the third trial, named Bertin, explains to us with much naiveté. The account which he gives before the tribunal is too instructive not to be quoted entire:

M. le Président: "Bertin, you may speak."

Bertin: "I am accused of belonging to a secret society. I deny it formally. I belong to the International, and I hope, in spite of all, to belong to it always. These are the circumstances in which I joined it: At the time of the strike of the iron-founders, we had a meeting; one of our friends said to us: 'We are on strike, we have constituted a society of resistance, but *we have still another thing to do, that is to belong to the International.*' This friend read us the statutes, we perceived that they were good and there was no inconvenience in belonging to it. A vote was taken, and *twelve hundred of us joined the International.* That happened the 28th of last April."

M. le Président: "Was this union according to rule?"

Bertin: "*The profession joined en masse.*"

---

* Letter quoted by the accusation in the third trial.

M. le Président: "Did you receive tickets?"

Bertin: "No one had any tickets."

M. le Président: "Are you subject to assessment?"

Bertin: "We have not had time to make it. In this meeting in which we joined *en masse* we said: 'We must not drag along slowly, we must organize immediately; let us nominate delegates for forming a section.' We named four delegates who went to the International and received all necessary information. Little books were given them containing the regulations of the International, and they were distributed, one for each workshop. I was one of the four delegates; it was in this capacity that I assisted at the reunions of the federal council, and it was there that I signed the manifesto."

Another accused, who was to acquire some months later a sad celebrity and pay with his life for his participation in the insurrection of March 18th, Duval, the future general of the Commune, explains in his turn in the same audience, with a language more violent and spiteful, but with motives absolutely identical, his entry into a society whose plots were very soon to lead him to death:

"In order to make the motives of our adhesion *en masse* to the International understood, I must here relate the beginning of our strike, that you may judge for yourselves whether our demands upon our employers were just and well founded. For several years day-wages have undergone such a diminution that two-thirds of the moulders were paid from four to five *francs*, while before this time day wages were five *francs* at the least; notwithstanding, it is easy to prove that the necessaries of life have increased on all sides; lodging, clothing, food, all have reached fabulous prices.

"In the winter of 1869–70, three-quarters of the foundries of Paris were worked only eight and nine hours a day; at last, the misery was at its height. At the end of the winter, it was decided in a reunion that these abuses must be made to cease at any cost; a committee was nominated for the purpose of studying the remedies in the business; after some meetings, this committee convoked the delegation of each workshop which accepted the plan, and the delegation having transmitted this statement to each workshop, it was adopted unanimously, except by a few voices.

"Thirty-six out of forty-seven of our employers refused; they received our demands with disdain, and some of them answered: *We will wait until you are hungry*. . . .

"In view of such contempt, the succeeding assembly voted and signed the strike to the *last;* they swore on their honor not to recommence before the complete acceptance of our demands; and *the proposition was made by me that all should join the International. Eight or nine hundred members present joined in a body*, signed their adhesion before breaking up, and nominated immediately four delegates to represent them at the general council of Paris.

"I was one of those delegates; Bertin was another. Now, sirs, I think I have sufficiently explained my joining the International."

The facts which Duval and Bertin recounted are the general rule; every strike, which led to a victory or a defeat, had as inevitable consequence the persuading of all the workingmen who took part in it to join the International.

How, therefore, can we believe the leaders of the association when they declare themselves scarcely partisans of these coalitions where they received their principal force?

II. STRIKE AT ROUBAIX IN 1867.—MANIFESTO OF THE INTERNATIONAL AND THE "JOURNAL DES DEBATS."

We have already been able to judge, upon a few facts quoted by us, with what ardor the International sustained strikes, and what importance it attached to not allowing the men whom it had pushed into the contest to return conquered to their workshops. A complete history of the coalitions to which it gave its support, and which have been able, thanks to it, either to win a complete victory or to make their employers pay dear for their defeats, would be almost the history of European industry itself for the last seven or eight years. Such a recital, if it were possible to make it, would lead us too far away; moreover, the majority of the documents which it would be necessary to have in hand in order to undertake it are not yet accessible. Probably, the trials made nearly everywhere of the members of the International who took part in the troubles and insurrections of that year, and the workingmen seized in their homes; later, the divisions which will result between the different sections, and the quarrels which will have preceded or followed them; the memoirs which several of the leaders will decide perhaps to write, all these diverse causes, and still many others, will initiate the public gradually into a crowd of mysteries which to-day are carefully concealed from it. Then it will be possible to write the complete history of the International, and particularly that of the strikes which it created. We can be sure that this will be one of the most curious and instructive pages in the annals of our century. But to-day we must submit on this point, as on many others of contemporaneous history, to merely throwing the dice near the point and endeavoring to guess what they try to conceal from us.

Perhaps they will have the kindness to give us, in place of a rapid nomenclature of the principal strikes, the detailed account of two or three of them, taken as types, in order to show the tragic incidents which too often occur to complicate them, and to bring to light what curious specimens of eloquence the publicists of the International displayed on such occasions.

It will be seen, also, by our account, that the movement of ideas which we remarked apropos of the congresses, was produced equally by reason of these coalitions. The violence of passions and of language increased from day to day, and the leaders who, in the first years, could in extreme cases allow themselves to blame officially the vices of their soldiers, were obliged, in the later times, to close their eyes upon their most reprehensible excesses, and to turn the thunders of their eloquence solely against the champions of order, guilty of having interposed to protect person and property.

In 1867, at Roubaix, new perfected machines were introduced which economized labor, for one man could conduct two at a time. The workingmen, thinking it just that they should share in the benefits which this improvement procured for the employers, claimed an increase of wages, which was refused them. The establishing of a new regulation, which imposed various fines as punishment for certain faults, increased the discontent. Their minds were much excited, and doubtless the leaders labored to increase this irritation, when on Saturday, March 16th, the storm, which for several days had muttered secretly, burst forth. The workingmen left their workshops abruptly in the middle of the day, crying out and offering menaces against different manufacturers. There were more than twenty-five thousand men who ran through the streets of the city, scattering fear everywhere by their vociferations. The municipal authority hastened to ask reinforcements from Lille. But before the summoned troops arrived, the disorder assumed serious proportions.

The workingmen, who for a long time had wandered through the streets without determined aim, finished by turning themselves, or rather by letting themselves be led, against the workshops designated for their vengeance. During several hours, scenes of pillage and devastation were created without its being possible to oppose the least resistance to the pillagers. Seven workshops were invaded, the machines were destroyed, the pieces of cloth on the frames slashed, and the chains cut upon the machines.

The private houses of two of the manufacturers, from whom most had been desired, were sacked; the furniture, beds, bedding, and dishes, were thrown out of the windows.

The rage of the rioters increased every moment, and they fired two of the workshops which they had devastated.

It is not known to what extent these madmen would have been carried if, that same evening, there had not arrived two battalions of the line and two squadrons of cuirassiers. The insurgents, faithful to the constant tactics of all these insurrections, received the soldiers with cries of: "*Vive la ligne!*" hoping thus to turn them from their duty; but, when they saw that these troops, instead of raising their guns in the air, charged arms, they decided to retire, and material order was rëestablished.

Sunday was not very bad; Monday, at six in the morning, many of the workingmen were at their work, and we can believe that the loiterers themselves came to resume their work at breakfast time. But all at once a word of command was given; immediately the weavers demanded an increase of wages, which was refused them; they retired, and a regular strike succeeded the outbreak, the opposite of what usually occurred; for most often, the coalition, at first peaceable, assumes only by degrees the character of an insurrection.

Whatever rôle the International played in the strike, or in the events which preceded it, it could not let facts so grave pass without making known officially the manner in which it judged them. In fact, MM. Tolain, Fribourg, and Varlin, in the character of *correspondents* of the committee of Paris, did not delay to publish the following manifesto:

"Much to be regretted troubles, accompanied by violence still more to be regretted, have broken out among the spinners and weavers of Roubaix.

"The causes are: 1st. The introduction of machines imposing upon the weavers an increase of work without an increase of pay, and cutting off at the same time a great number of workingmen; 2nd. The establishment of a regulation imposing measures offensive to their dignity and fines which were flagrant violations of law; 3rd. Finally, the intervention of the *gendarmerie* in these details of private interests, and in a case where it ought perhaps to watch over the public security, but not to protect by its presence the pretensions of individuals.

"The strike provoked by these causes has had for consequences, sad events of which public opinion has been informed.

"In this situation, the International Association considers it its duty to declare itself, and to call the attention of workingmen of all countries by making the following declarations;

"The use of machines in industry raises an economic problem, whose speedy solution is imperiously demanded. We, workingmen, recognize on principle the right of workingmen to a proportionate increase of salary, when, by new implements, a more considerable production is imposed upon them.

"In France, land of universal suffrage and equality, the workman is still citizen when he has crossed the threshold of the workshop or the manufactory. The regulations imposed upon the spinners of Roubaix, are made for slaves and not for free men. They threaten not only the dignity, but even the existence of the workingmen, since the amount of taxes may cut off and exceed the rates of salary.

"In an equal debate, when no violence had been committed, and the strike commenced by the abandonment of the workshops, the intervention of the *gendarmerie* could only irritate the workingmen who thought they beheld pressure and threats.

"Workingmen of Roubaix, whatever your just grievances may be, nothing can justify the acts of destruction of which you have been guilty,—consider that the machine, the instrument of labor, should be sacred to you; consider that such violence compromises your cause and that of all laborers;—consider that you have just furnished arms to the adversaries of liberty and the calumniators of the people.

"The strike continues: new arrests have been made. We remind every member of the International Association of Workingmen, that there are at this moment brothers at Roubaix who are suffering. If there are among them men, who for one moment led astray, were guilty of violence which we condemn, there is between them and us solidarity of interest and misery; at the bottom of the contest, there are also just grievances which the manufacturers should remove. Finally, there are families without a head; let each one of us bring to them moral and material aid."

We see that the representatives of the International while they accuse the employers on every point, recognized at least that the workingmen on their part had committed excesses to be regretted, and that they did not hesitate to blame them.

Le Journal des Débats published on this subject, under the signature of the editorial secretary, an article which we cannot reproduce here entire, because of its length, but from which we must quote at least a part:

"The events at Roubaix have given rise to a manifestation which can not be passed over in silence; this is a declaration of the *International Association of Workingmen*, represented by three members of the Committee of Paris, who sign themselves with the title of *Correspondents:* MM. Tolain, Fribourg, and Varlin. The International Association of Workingmen is little known to our readers, but it is well that it is so, although it seems to us only to exist yet in an experimental or embryonic state. It aspires to nothing less than the embracing of the workingmen of all manufacturing trades of Europe, and it is certain that it has some numerous ramifications already in England and on the

Continent. It will then be the largest society which has ever been formed. It has been seen on occasion of the strike which lately suspended in Paris the bronze trade, that the principal object of this association will be to interfere in times of strikes, sustaining not only by its influence, but also by its subsidies, the unoccupied workingmen of the trade in which the strike shall have been declared.

"The International Association had at least a word to say on the subject of what has transpired at Roubaix, since these much to be regretted events had their origin in a strike. This is what it has done through the medium of the three *correspondents* whom we have just quoted. It condemns the violence of which some misguided men were guilty. It warns the workingmen in general that such violence compromises the cause of all laborers. It declares that the machine, as an instrument of labor, should be sacred. These are salutary and opportune truths. Unfortunately the preambles are not equal to the enacting part. According to the letter of the *correspondents*, up to the time of the destructions of the machines and the sack of the workshops, all the wrong doing was on the side of the employers. These wrongdoings are enumerated in the letter, and the enumeration merits consideration."

After having discussed not only with impartiality but even with good will towards the three signers of the manifesto, the different reproaches which they addressed to the employers, the anonymous author of this article turns around upon them and shows them that public opinion demanded that they should have explained themselves in their turn ; then he returns to MM. Tolain, Fribourg, and Varlin, and throws light, on one side, upon that which is praiseworthy in their publication ; and on the other, that which he regrets not to find there :

"Although the *correspondents* of the International association may have applied themselves especially in their manifesto to setting off in relief the wrongdoings which they attributed to the employers, a certain courage was necessary in order to blame, as they have done, the disorders of Roubaix. Their language of condemnation is not without energy ; there might, however, have been more of it. It is not necessary to say to the workingmen : The causes of the strike and of that which follows was the presence of the *gendarmes* in the manufactories, the introduction of the new frames, the establishment of a more severe regulation in the manufactories ; it was necessary to tell them that the cause of the sad events, the cause not accidental or secondary, but predominant, was the ignorance of the workingmen concerning their own interests, and the weakness with which a certain number of them abandoned themselves to evil propensities. It would have been wiser to represent to the population that if they had better habits, if they abandoned the public-houses, far too much frequented in the North, they would no longer be, nearly as much, at the mercy of incidents which can suspend work. The *correspondents* of the International association would have done better in the rôle of intelligent leaders and honest guides if they had said to the workingmen : 'You are ignorant, inform yourselves. Profit by the facilities which are given you to-day to instruct yourselves. Many of you lack sobriety ; let them correct themselves ; let them work six days in the week ; let them thus acquire some savings for slack seasons. The workingmen of Northern Germany have no higher salaries than you, and yet they have furnished the funds for 900 or 1,000 banks of the people, which are formed on the model recommended by M. Schultze-Delitsch, banks which are at the same time conducted like the savings banks and institutions of credit.' The *correspondents* of the International association attach a great value to strengthening and extending the authority which they exercise over their fellow-members ; authority, in order to justify its prerogative, has sometimes need to speak the whole truth, however painful it may be to hear it."

The *correspondents* of the International replied to the *Journal des Débats* by a long letter, in which they did little but resume and develop each of the points considered in the first manifesto ; the *Journal des Débats* inserted it without making a response, which nothing, in fact, rendered necessary, and the discussion rested there.

Upon the whole, the men who spoke in the name of the International, had, in their manifesto, flattered the bad passions of the workingmen of Roubaix, and advanced either knowingly, for the needs of their cause, or unwittingly and by themselves being deceived, statements completely false, when they attributed the pillage and incendiarism of the workshops to the intervention of the *gendarmerie;* but, finally, they dared to blame these scenes of devastation; that was much.

The journal which represents more than any other French sheet to the eyes of the public the high, rich, and cultivated *bourgeoisie,* had discussed their proclamation by marking the tendencies already too evident of their society, but in a tone calm, courteous, and even well-wishing. MM. Tolain, Fribourg, and Varlin, who thought it their duty to respond to these criticisms, did it without too far exceeding the moderation of which an example had been given them.*

---

* These pages were already written when we found in *Le Soir,* of July 19th, an article in which M. Fribourg, one of the signers of this manifesto, relates as follows the affair of Roubaix and the intervention of the *correspondents* of the association:

"About the same time, a terrible incident occurred: the workingmen of Roubaix, in a burst of furious rage, broke the machines, burned the workshops, maltreated the innocent; a cry of deserved condemnation rose in the ranks of the *bourgeoisie;* the workingmen were silent, thunderstruck; their consciences forbade them to applaud, but they lacked energy to condemn.

"Only the Internationals, risking their growing popularity, dared to raise their voices to condemn energetically such remonstrances, and in a public letter addressed to the strikers of Roubaix, they thus expressed themselves:

"WORKINGMEN OF ROUBAIX:

"Whatever may be your just grievances, nothing can justify the acts of destruction of which you have been guilty; consider that machinery, the instrument of labor, should be sacred to you; consider that such violence compromises your cause and that of all

Let us see now how they expressed themselves two years later, in circumstances very similar, in the official publications of the International.

III. STRIKE OF SERAING IN 1869.—MANIFESTO OF THE GENERAL BELGIAN COUNCIL.

The 2nd of April, a strike burst out among the puddlers and stokers of the "iron manufactory" of the Cockerill Society of Seraing. The principal motives of the strike were the claims relative to the number of *charges* or *heats* demanded of them in a day's work, and the discussions upon the subject of the length of this day.

After some conferences, difficulties seemed settled by means of concessions made on both sides, particularly an increase of wages, and the readmission into the manufactory of a workman who had

---

laborers; consider that you have just furnished arms to the adversaries of liberty and the calumniators of the people.

TOLAIN, FRIBOURG, VARLIN,
Correspondents of Paris.

"The workingmen of Paris applauded this language, and the association acquired by this courageous act a considerable moral influence."

We see that M. Fribourg blamed much more vigorously in 1871, as associate editor of *Le Soir*, the *furious lunatics* of Roubaix, than he did in 1867, as *correspoudent* of the Paris section of the International. We see particularly that he singularly reduced the text of his manifesto to the workingmen of Roubaix, and that he carefully holds back all the passages in which he did wrong in flattering the passions of these *furious lunatics*, and in excusing their crimes by throwing the responsibility upon the intervention of the *gendarmerie.*

been sent away a little while before for an act of strike.

No disorder had taken place up to this time.

Le Reveil of Seraing, giving an account of this first day of hostilities at the time in which peace was thought to be definitely concluded, closed its recital with the following lines:

"The day of the strike, the International received 250 adhesions: it received them on condition of their abstaining from all violent manifestations, of exposing their grievances with decorum, and of demanding nothing but justice. They promised this unanimously, and have kept their promise: upon this we congratulate them.

We will see presently in what way the International was, in truth, the jealous observer of decorum and especially of moderation.

The workmen returned to their work. "During four days," says *L'Internationale* of April 18th, "most perfect calm reigned in the manufactory. It was because care had been taken to remove the hated overseer. The workmen believed themselves already freed from his tyranny, when they saw him reappear with the director, who declared that those who were not satisfied with his return had only to go elsewhere. Immediately all the puddlers left work. The director was not alarmed; for he had not wasted his time during these four days of temporizing; he had provided iron all prepared which permitted him to do without the puddlers. The noble conduct of the workmen frustrated this jesuitical manoeuvre; the stokers and the flatteners declared that they were associated in the lot of the puddlers, and the iron manufactory of M. John Cockerill was deserted."

In this recital, borrowed from an official journal of the great association, we can easily guess what had in reality transpired.

The International wished a strike of the puddlers; it did not succeed the first time, and the workmen came to an understanding with their employer; but it had its revenge.

The return of this hated overseer was only a pretext, for in the account of *Le Reveil* of Seraing, written between the first resumption of work and its new interruption, all the grievances of the workmen are complacently enumerated and commented upon at length; notwithstanding there is no allusion made to the claims against any overseer whatever.

But this time the International succeeded too completely. It had, according to all probability, desired and fomented a partial strike; for it is its interest to have the fewest mouths possible to feed. The concessions demanded by the workmen on strike once wrested from their employers, they are almost always imposed without contest on all the other heads of the same trade. Nothing is more naturally indicated than these tactics; and we have proof that this is, in effect, the system habitually preferred by the leaders of the association. "I ought," writes Varlin to Aubry, October 8th, 1869, apropos of a strike at Elbeuf, "I ought to counsel you to prevent the extension of the strike to other manufactories in the environs of Elbeuf. If the employers do not constrain it, *let the workmen have patience and wait, in order to demand the tariff, which may be obtained in the houses actually on strike.*"*

---

* Are new proofs desired of the evil which the simultaneousness of important strikes did to the International? Let one read the following passages from various letters of Varlin to Aubry, quoted by the imperial advocate in the third trial (audience of June 22nd, 1870.)

PARIS, NOVEMBER 4, 1869.

"MY DEAR AUBRY:

"I send you inclosed 800 *francs*, of which 300 *francs* as second loan from the Society of Bronzers and 500 *francs* as subscriptions. But I must tell you with regret that, for this week, this is all that I can send you; I surpass even the amount of subscriptions received up to this day.

"We are at this time in an excessively difficult situation, on account of the strike of the leather-dressers, which has become general during the last week and numbers a thousand strikers. The delegates of the Paris societies, in the general assemblies of the leather-dressers, have urged to a general strike and have promised the moral and material aid of all the societies. We are then, all the Paris societies, engaged in the affair. It is not only the leather-dressers who fight against their employers, but all the workingmen's societies of Paris.

"Now, in the financial situation in which we find ourselves at this moment, we must make a supreme effort: also I have not been at all for a week in a condition to obtain loans, and I do not believe it possible for me to risk new demands next week. As for the subscription, one has been opened for the leather-dressers; ours will be stopped now, after having been fettered at its beginning, by that in favor of the victims of Aubin. In view of the gravity of this situation, I have written to Brussels and to Berlin, but Brussels does not respond; meanwhile my letter should have arrived eight days ago already. Have they written to you? You say nothing to me of it.

"As for Berlin, it was only last Monday that I wrote to the federation of the workingmen's societies of La Salle of Germany. I

The leaders of the strike of Seraing wished to follow this system which ordinarily succeeded; but the efforts which they made to conduct the strike of the puddlers had also caused an ebullition of the other workmen, little understanding, in fact, indus-

---

supported my demand through the section of democratic German socialists of Paris: I hope for a good result, but that can not be until next week.

(Signed,) E. VARLIN."

PARIS, NOVEMBER 8, 1869.

"MY DEAR AUBRY:

"I am obliged to write you a few words, in order to acquaint you with the situation in which we find ourselves here, and to warn you in time that you cannot count upon Paris this week, that you may make a new effort among the other sections to raise the amounts which you need.

"I have already told you of the strike of the leather-dressers and of the difficult situation in which it places us.

"We had thought that the strike could not last more than eight days because of the considerable quantity of goods in manufacture (about one million), and which must be completely lost if it remains in suspense a fortnight or three weeks at the most. It was hoped that the employers would yield if the first payment was completely made, for the employers thought that they would not find the sum in four days. 8,000 *francs* were needed; the first payment has been made, but the employers have not yielded: a new general assembly of the leather-dressers, new assurances from the delegates; then, after the assembly, reunion of the delegates for consideration. There was needed for Sunday, yesterday, 12,000 *francs*. In ordinary times this sum would be raised easily enough, but to-day the *treasuries are exhausted.* However, it was nearly raised, and the payment was made yesterday, but at the cost of some effort!

"To-day we are preparing for the payment for next Sunday. *The societies give their last funds, selling their last stock*; the subscription in the workshops is pushed to the utmost, and to turn all into money, we are going to have a public reunion this week upon the question of actual strikes, for we must not forget that besides the leather-dressers we have the paint-brush makers on strike for six weeks; the canvass-weavers for eight weeks; the wood-gilders for trial strategy. "Unfortunately," says the official journal of the association, "the workmen, laboring in the Cockerill coal mines, placed themselves equally on strike, in spite of the wise recommendations of the members of the International of Se-

---

a fortnight, and all the wool-weavers whom we do not absolutely forget. If some of our strikes terminate, we can still aid you; but you must see that at this time all our efforts are for Paris.

"Already, several times, I have been asked if it were not possible to obtain something from the provinces or from foreigners. But I replied that the province was sustaining you; as for foreigners, you know my proceedings. Up to to-day, no result.

"*(Signed,)* E. VARLIN."

PARIS, NOVEMBER 16, 1869.

"MY DEAR AUBRY:

"I send you enclosed 200 *francs* of a subscription which I have received since last week.

"Our situation is ever the same.

"The leather-dressers' strike continues, in spite of the considerable losses sustained by the employers. We know from a sure source that all the members of the paternal syndical hide and leather chamber have united to sustain this strike, that is to say, that they indemnify the leather-dressers' employers for the losses which they undergo.

"It hardly seems possible to us, that all the syndical chambers of employers, which compose what they call the National Union of Commerce and Trade, are leagued to ruin workingmen's societies, by making them exhaust their treasuries by several interminable strikes, for we have never had one of this length.

"After seven weeks of contest, the paint-brush makers succumbed last week. The societies which had at first sustained them had to abandon them so as to centralize all their efforts in favor of the leather dressers.

Finally, Varlin writes to Aubry, December 2nd:

"We have already paid out 51,000 *francs* for the leather-dressers, and yet since the first week, we have been always short of funds."

The manufacturers who wish to establish a serious resistance against the International, cannot consider too much these letters and all those of the same kind quoted in the course of the trial, raing, who endeavored to show them the untimeliness of this measure. Other coal-mines followed this example, among others that of *L'Espérance.* Until this time nothing mischievous had occurred; but the lords of these places, who become mad with fear when they see four workmen united, (sign that their conscience is a little troubled), brought the troops, and, as always, they brought with them disorder and massacre."

We have seen at Roubaix, in 1867, what evil a misguided crowd can do in a few hours, when there are no troops at hand. As soon as the soldiers protect order, the rights and life of peaceable citizens, they are butchers hired by the oppressors of the people.

At Seraing, it was not even to protect the manufactories and their shops, but to defend themselves that the soldiers were constrained to use their arms. It is not from the *bourgeois* journals that we ask the proof of this, but from *L'Internationale* itself; for the truth shows itself plainly in its recital through the falsehoods under which it tried to smother it. It is "the companion Eugène Hins," one of the principal leaders of the association in Belgium, who himself relates the events in the official sheet of the society.

"On Friday evening, a numerous mob was stationed in Cockerill street. Was there provocation on the part of the mob? Were stones thrown at the first? We do not know; but we will say that *if the troops had not shown themselves very useless, the stones would not have been thrown,* and afterwards if, among some hundreds of persons, *some rash ones threw stones*, that is no reason for condemning the others.

" *The three usual summons were given.* Nothing so odious as this manner of assuming an appearance of legality. Can a compact mob thus disperse in a few minutes? Then the people do not yet believe sufficiently in the perversity of its rulers, it believes always that their threats are in sport.

"At this time it was dark night (10 o'clock). Two smoky street-lamps did not suffice to pierce the darkness. All at once the cavalry moved forward and swept through the middle of the street, while the infantry, crossing bayonets, ran along the sidewalks.

" Judge of the carnage which must be made in this compact crowd, struck before having been able to flee.

" It is impossible to estimate the number of the wounded, but it must have been very considerable. As for the dead, two are reported; but how many unfortunates may have died in by-places!

" These same scenes were renewed on the morrow; they have been related to me by two victims."

The association could not let escape so happy an occasion for making new recruits. Thus it sums up all the means at its disposal:

" We met at Lize," says Eugène Hins in the course of his recital, " the companions Adrien and Varlet, arrived from Verviers, who sold bravely, in the face of the *gendarmes*, the accounts of the strike of Hodimont. They believed with reason that the dignified attitude held by the workingmen of Verviers, in this circumstance, would exert a happy influence over the workingmen of Seraing."

The delegates of the International of Liége and Brussels took counsel with those of Seraing, and decided that they must hasten to call a meeting:

"A considerable crowd answered this invitation. The hall, which can contain from a thousand to twelve hundred persons, was full. The companions Lepourgen (of Seraing), Hins, and Adrien had the floor and after having pledged the workingmen present not to yield to oppression, they showed them, nevertheless, that they ought not to remain stationary, but labor to prepare for the future in the heart of the International."

Other companions afterwards spoke in the same manner; after which, "the companions Hins and Lepourgen encouraged the puddlers to yield nothing of their just claims, but exerted themselves to obtain from the miners a promise that they would return to work on the morrow, that they might procure resources for sustaining their brothers.

"If they did not wholly succeed in the sense that the workmen of the Cockerill trenches declared that they would persist, at least the workmen of the other mines promised to return to work on the morrow. We have since learned that they kept their promise, a very important result, as it limited the strike."

From the account even of the official journal of the association it is easy to extricate the truth.

The strike, without doubt fomented and ordered

by the International, but with the formal design of localizing it that it might be more easily sustained, broke out in the Cockerill works.

The workmen of different coal-mines of Seraing also quitted work, in spite of the wish of the International, which did not desire to have too many mouths to feed at once, for fear that its resources would be exhausted before the victory of the strikers.

The increasing excitement of the population of Seraing obliged the Belgian government to send troops to protect life and property. The troops which arrived found themselves exposed to insults and attacks, which obliged them to thrust back the mob, but without using their fire-arms.

The cavalry made some charges in the middle of the streets; the infantry at the same time cleared the sidewalks, advancing with charged bayonets.

Two workmen were killed in this fray; several persons received some wounds and contusions more or less serious.

The International profits by these events for pushing propagandism more actively than ever, scattering its pamphlets and uniting in meetings the workingmen excited by the contest against their employers and the conflicts with the army.

Then, when the minds were thought to be sufficiently inflamed by these events, by these speeches, by these meetings, the general Belgian council issues the following address "to the workingmen of Seraing and its environs:"

"COMPANIONS:

"At all times grief and misery have been the destiny of the laborer; at all times the people have groaned in the presence of their masters' joy, have been hungry in the presence of the satiety of those speculating upon them.

"But man is so made that he becomes accustomed to everything, even to the severest privations. The chain continues to weigh upon him, but he bears it without murmuring; he has lost even the sentiment of hatred; then, he is truly a slave, for he no longer feels the disgrace of his slavery.

"This, companions, is the unfortunate state into which many of our workingmen are actually reduced; it is this inertia which gives force to our tyrants. But there are those unfortunates, pushed to extremities, who having until then suffered without murmuring, make their claims heard. Their masters are astonished at such audacity; they tremble as the spirit of independence spreads among the laboring class, and in order to stifle this monster in its cradle, they attack with sabres, guns, and grape-shot. But now, there happens what these men without heart could not prevent; it happens instead of the profound silence which they thought would succeed to the massacre, that indignant clamors arise on all sides; that hatred awakens in the hearts of the people, and they are there, upright, raging, ready to shake off their chains.

"Companions of Seraing, as during three whole nights the soldiery has sabred and pierced, often without any provocation, we raised this cry of indignation, when we learned of your wrongs; we felt hatred taking hold of us, and truly, if action had followed the thought, in the first moment we would have desired the destruction of your barbarous exterminators.

"But, companions, when reflection had succeeded to the first movement of such lawful indignation, we found ourselves plunged in another current of ideas.

"How many times the workingmen, driven to extremities, have sworn the ruin of their oppressors, and, after a fleeting triumph, have fallen back more than ever into slavery!

"It is not sufficient to destroy, one must rebuild, and one cannot build in a day.

"Restrain then, a moment, companions, your lawful indignation, and do not reply to the provocations of the army.

"Consider that your masters would ask nothing better than to see you answer violence by violence, so as to have a pretext for still more sanguinary oppression. Consider that your brothers of other parts of the country have not yet all comprehended the necessity for throwing off their chains, and that a series of successive revolts could only lead to a series of successive defeats.

"Consider that, even when all the workingmen in Belgium have an understanding to make their cause triumph, they will be powerless as long as in the large states of Europe despotism shall be enthroned triumphant upon the dead bodies of its victims.

"Consider, finally, that the revolt leads to nothing; that it is necessary that the revolution be prepared, that in the day in which it shall be triumphant, it must be able, almost without a blow, to substitute a new order of things in the place of the former order, which is no longer that of disorder.

"Therefore, companions, be calm; maintain your legitimate pretensions, but do not let yourselves be led into violence. Learn to wait, your day will come.

"*Join en masse the International Association of workingmen;* there you will learn your rights, and the means which you must employ to make them triumph; there you will unite with your brothers of all parts of the country and of the whole world. And, when all the workingmen's forces shall be united and instructed as to what they are to do, on that day, from all points of the world at once, the workingmen will make their voice heard, which will make iniquity totter and inaugurate justice. On that day, companions, we will no longer say to you, Be calm; we will shout to you, *Forward!*

"Until then, be patient and await your time.

"THE GENERAL BELGIAN COUNCIL.

"BRUSSELS, APRIL 13TH, 1869."

It suffices to compare this document with that which we quoted several pages previous, in order to see how the passions had developed in two years in the International.

In 1867, the *correspondents* of the Paris sections without doubt excited with all their might their associates against the employers and against the government, but while spreading out before them ideas false and violent, they nevertheless recommended moderation in their actions. In 1869, the general Belgian council promised its faithful servants that they very soon would have the power all to themselves, that they would be the masters of society, and if it exhorted them still to have patience, it was only in order that when the moment came, they could with an irresistible force and without danger for themselves, give society the final blow.

If we cannot praise either the ideas or the sentiments of the authors of this proclamation, we must at least take their frankness kindly.

We must in finishing this account repeat what we said in commencing it.

If we have described the strike of Roubaix and that of Seraing rather than any other, it is not because they differed from others in anything, but because we wished to show by two examples the most common incidents, the most frequent episodes of these sad industrial wars.

There are scarcely any years in which we do not find a certain number of these large strikes which agitate whole populations, which starve the workingmen by thousands, which threaten with complete ruin a number more or less considerable leaders of trade, and which too often lead to bloody conflicts between the strikers who have become insurgents and the army called to protect the life and the property of the citizens.

Aubin and La Ricamarie have left a mournful remembrance, because the chassepot which had already "done wonders" at Mentana, according to the unfortunate expression of General Failly, made then its first appearance in civil troubles, and its effects were terrible ; but aside from these details interesting for a history of fireworks or the families of the victims, the strikes of Aubin and La Ricamarie were not more remarkable than those of Roubaix and Seraing, than fifty or a hundred strikes that we might just as well have chosen.

Let us add also that the intervention of the bayonet and the chassepot is happily needless ordinarily, and that the largest number of strikes, even those which caused the most damage to the two belligerent parties were terminated without shedding of blood.

But, since 1854, few have been seen which have terminated without bringing adherents to the International by hundreds or thousands.

CHAPTER IX.

THE INTERNATIONAL AND THE EMPIRE.

I. THE PARTIES IN 1864.—THE REVOLUTIONARY PARTY: THE JACOBINS AND THE SOCIALISTS.—THE FOUNDERS OF THE INTERNATIONAL DECIDE THAT THE ASSOCIATION SHALL REMAIN A STRANGER TO POLITICS.

At the time in which the International was founded, the Empire was still in all its power, and although the fatal war of Mexico had created already very serious difficulties for it, it was scarcely possible to foresee then to what a deep and irremediable fall the weight of its faults would drag it down, in the course of a few years.

No one of the parties which fought against it seemed at that time to have serious chances of success; no one of them especially shared the passions and aspirations of the founders of the new society.

The Legitimist party, composed almost exclusively of large proprietors, equally devoted to the interests of the church and to those of the monarchy, almost as hostile to democracy as to demagogism, was naturally still more opposed than the Bonapartists themselves to the guests of the banquet of Saint Martin's Hall, and to the delegates assembled at Geneva.

The Orleanists had without doubt very little taste for the Empire, which regarded them, not without reason, as its most dangerous enemies ; but if they were friends for the most part of the liberties which the socialist claimed loudly in ordinary times, reserving their suppression until they thought themselves strongest, they held also very energetically to order ; they were very decided never to sacrifice one of the grand principles without which modern society could not exist. Moreover, they nearly all belonged to the élite of liberal profession, to the most enlightened, most active, most industrious and richest *bourgeoisie*, to what was most honorable and most intelligent in the financial and industrial world, that is to say, to all the social categories which the growing association regarded with the most envy and hate.

Finally, there existed a party which seemed at first a natural ally of the International, the republican party, but neither of the two different parts of which it was composed had much more attraction for it than the other.

The moderate Republicans, those whom the most advanced call formalist Republicans, that is to say, those who were on marvellously good terms with the liberal conservative party, as soon as the word republic had been substituted for the word monarchy in the name of the government, very naturally were kindled by the same distrust or rather by the same aversion against the practical socialists of the new society as the Orleanists.

The extreme Republicans, on the contrary, Jacobins, Montagnards, Hébertistes and Babouvistes, Radicals, eternally irreconcilable, whom no change satisfied, who must belong to a conspiracy or die, who love revolution for the sake of revolution as the Romanticists of 1830 loved art "for the sake of art:" these everlastingly furious men who could not accommodate themselves any more easily to the provisional government of February 24th than to that of Charles X. or of Louis Philippe, who execrated the *Constituante* of 1848 as much as the undiscoverable chamber of 1816, and saw in General Cavaignac, a direct successor of "Polignac;" these men ought, it seemed, to be very dear to the International; and no one would be astonished to see these two parties form a close alliance for making the attack upon society, reserving the right to disagree on the morrow of the victory. However, this union, which seemed made before having been proposed, was on the contrary almost impossible, thanks to the difficulties of character common to the two parties called to form it.

The very essence of the demagogic mind, is distrust. M. About, in one of his prettiest stories, describes an old soldier, who had been dead fifty years, whom a savant resuscitated by a process of his own invention. The first idea of this brave officer on coming to life was to call for his newspaper. If the *man with the broken ear* had been a good revolutionist, a true *pure,* his first cry would have been; "We are betrayed!" The Internationals are almost Jacobins in this respect; this disposition common to both parties already rendered harmony difficult between them.

Moreover, they were separated by still another

barrier: almost all the Jacobins are waifs from the middle classes, and the perfume of the demagogism which they exhaled was spoiled for the nose of a true *International* by I know not what odor of *bourgeoisie.* The veritable socialists condemned Louis XVI. and Robespierre to the same execution, the one as chief of the aristocracy, and the other as leader of the "*bourgeois* reaction."

It is true that the Jacobins, the *Pures,* could neither say to the others, nor acknowledge to themselves, that they only conspired for the love of conspiracy, that they raised barricades for the pleasure which the sight of stones piled up gave them, and that they invoked civil war because of the lively satisfaction which they experienced in hearing the roll of the drums and the rattling of the firing. Consequently, they were obliged to adopt and publish a programme, and their programme does not differ sensibly, at least to the eye of a *bourgeois,* from that of a member of the International. It was not enough for them to demand a *republic,* they wished it to be *democratic,* it need not be said, and *social* into the bargain, as they call themselves socialists just like the others; but the others felt that this was only a concession to opinion, and that this socialism was not proof against everything.

The organ of the International at Geneva, *L'Egalité,* was not deceived by it.

"Propagandism interested, and at the highest point corrupter of priests, governments, and all political *bourgeois* parties, without excepting the extreme Reds, has spread a mass of false ideas among the laboring masses, and these blind masses become impassioned unfortunately too often by means of falsehoods which have no end but to make them serve voluntarily and stupidly, the interests of privileged classes to the detriment of their own.

"The slavery and misery of the people will always remain the same as long as the popular masses continue to serve as instruments to the *bourgeois* policy, so long as this policy is called conservative, liberal, progressive, radical, and even *when it assumes the most revolutionary manners of the world.* For every *bourgeois* policy, whatever may be its color or its name, can only have at bottom one end: the maintenance of *bourgeois* domination; and the *bourgeois* domination, is the slavery of the proletariat."

Thus, all the parties which it found organized were equally objects of suspicion or hatred to the International, and it was as difficult for it to decide to unite with one as with another.

These were motives serious enough to induce the association to abstain from mixing itself up in political questions. Other considerations which they could not develop in their journals or their meetings, remained still to compel the leaders to advise and even at the first to command this wise abstinence.

As we have just related, the empire was or rather seemed very strong. Without the connivance or at least the tolerance of the imperial government, it was almost impossible for the association to develop itself seriously in France. Now, the Emperor had been proclaimed, it is true, for fear of socialism, and if the author of the 2nd of December had been permitted to suppress all liberty, it was because he had promised to profit by this unlimited authority to overwhelm socialism ; but he failed as completely in this engagement as in those which he had undertaken against the king Louis-Philippe and against the republic. The decree of February 17th, which submitted the press to the most absolute control, served only to protect the personal interests of the members of the imperial family and of the principal personages of the state at the same time as the financial interests of the highest placed stock-jobbers and the least scrupulous speculators; but they cared very little to defend the society which they had sworn to save, and the Emperor, who had a great love for all innovations, did not deny a certain leaning toward social reforms.

In such a situation, to incur from the first his ill will, then all powerful, by declaring itself friendly to the republic, would have been the most marked madness on the part of the founders of the association. On the other hand, to seek his protection, and his favors at the cost of an official adhesion to the empire, or even more simply, by means of some flatteries more or less delicate, or some electoral compliances, could not be thought of, for all the adherents, fanatically hostile to the empire, because it was the established government, would have deserted the new society *en masse* after the first steps taken in this course by its leaders.

Accordingly, only one thing was possible : to lay

down the principle of the preëminence of social questions over political questions and to declare that they would hold themselves absolutely aloof from all politics: this is what was done, and they remained so very faithful to this programme during the earlier days, that the ministers of the empire, hoping always to gain this growing power by some favors, had the simplicity to permit it to develop in all freedom during the time when it would have been possible to crush it.

The statesmen of the empire disdained, as a proof of narrowness of mind, a policy upright and loyal and faithful to its engagements. They considered themselves profound politicians, when they put Prussia at enmity with Austria in order to seize the Rhenish provinces when once the two adversaries should have exhausted themselves; they regarded themselves as little Machiavellis when they let the International increase in order to make use of it against the *bourgeoisie* always enamored of liberty and control. The Emperor could appreciate September 2d at Sedan, and the Empress September 4th at Paris, the usefulness of this grand policy, so disdainful of the precepts of the petty *bourgeois* honesty.

But let us return to our actual subject, to the history of the relations of the International with the empire, and with the various divisions of the revolutionary party.

II. FIRST RELATIONS BETWEEN THE INTERNATIONAL AND THE IMPERIAL GOVERNMENT.—M. ROUHER SOLICITS AN INTERVIEW.—HE ASKS COMPLIMENTS FOR THE EMPEROR.—THE INTERNATIONAL MAKES OVERTURES TO THE JACOBINS.—FIRST HOSTILITIES.—MANIFESTATION ON THE BOULEVARD MONTMARTRE.—RUPTURE WITH THE DEPUTIES OF THE SEINE.—FIRST AND SECOND TRIAL OF THE INTERNATIONAL.

As soon as the plan of the association was decided upon at London in 1864, the organizers were eager to open at Paris, as we have already said, a " bureau of correspondence " and to invite " the workingmen " to adhere to the provisory statutes. " But," says M. Murat in his defense before the Imperial Court of Paris, (audience of April 22d,) " the Paris *correspondents*, members of the general council sitting at London, did not think themselves obliged to ask authorization; they did not create an association in the interior, they invited adhesions to an international association, having its seat in a foreign country; they then simply made,—in order to attest that they, nevertheless, intended to assume all the responsibility of the acts of this association at Paris,—a declaration to the prefect of the police and one to the minister of the interior, of the opening of the bureau; they inclosed a copy of the provisory statutes drawn up at the meeting at London."

The prefect and the minister received the declaration and responded neither by a formal prohibition nor a regular authorization. "If," continues M. Murat, "after the declarations made to the administrative authorities and the police, the *correspondents* had received notice, as had happened in other cases, that this was not sufficient; that an *express* authorization, as the court says, was necessary, they would have thought of another manner of proceeding; but, let us say it boldly, they never could have brought themselves to the idea of submitting to the humiliation of authorization."

The government, on its side, adduced considerations of the highest order for explaining the expectant attitude which it had at first taken towards the growing society, then the rigorous measures to which it at last decided to have recourse.

We have a right, to-day, to seek, under the lofty phrases of both parties, the real motive of their conduct; it is not difficult to discover, and we have already exposed it. The empire hoped either to find in the association founded at Saint Martin's Hall a support against the *bourgeoisie*, or to make use of it as a bug-bear to check the liberal aspirations which already began to burst out everywhere in the middle classes; the leaders of the International guessed, perhaps, this policy, saw in every case the good intentions, which, for one reason or another were felt towards them, and hastened to profit by them, glad to escape, at the time when they were yet feeble and isolated, a contest in which their society might perish.

However, it was impossible to remain thus everlastingly under observation. "The growing power of the International, which showed itself in the strikes of Roubaix, Amiens, Paris, Geneva, etc.," (says the report of the general council at the congress of Brussels,) "put the government to the necessity of *absorbing or destroying it.* The empire chose, at first, to be satisfied with little. The manifesto of the Parisians read at the Geneva congress, having been stopped on the French frontier, our bureau of Paris demanded of the minister of the interior the motives for this seizure. *M. Rouher solicited an interview* in which he consented to authorize the admission of the manifesto." But he consented on condition that some modifications should be made; on the refusal of the Paris members, he added: "However, if you will return a few thanks in the address to the Emperor, who has done so much for the laboring classes, we will see." "These words excited in the congress," we quote the author of the account which we have before our eyes, a "general hilarity." M. Eugène Dupont, the reporter, adds immediately: "The sub-Emperor, M. Rouher, made this his condition," and this phrase was received with "prolonged applause."

In spite of the prudence of both opponents, war became inevitable. Certain incidents did not hinder its bursting out. The old revolutionary party, of which Mazzini, Garibaldi, Blanqui, and Ledru-Rollin, were the gods, saw with distrust the founding of the International; it was naturally thought that the newcomers were the traitors. When it heard them declare that they would abstain from handling politics properly so-called, it cried "treason" more loudly, and these cries disquieted a sufficiently large number of the members of the International, divided between their revolutionary instincts and their social instincts. The prudence of the leaders which preserved them from prosecutions from above, exposed them to all the suspicions from below. The official subsidies which had facilitated their journey to London in 1862, were condemned with violence: it was remarked with sharpness that no one of them had been compromised in the affair of the coffee-house of *La Renaissance* which had sent to prison for several months Protot, Tridon, Landowski, Villeneuve, Jeunesse, and the flower of the Jacobin demagogy (January, 1867): also the entire mass of the adherents of the International began to be disquieted, and exerted upon its chiefs a pressure more and more strong to induce them to *affirm* the democratic principles of the association.

In 1867, the congress of Lausanne voted energetic resolutions against the war. Now, at the very same time, in Geneva, that is to say, only a few leagues from the city where the International was holding its sittings, the other division of the demagogic party, under the pretext of forming a *congress of peace,* declared war against all tyrants, all oppressors of the people, and thanks to the exploits of the orators who were hardly agreed among themselves, the electoral palace where these meetings were held, became each day more and more worthy of its picturesque surname of *box on the ears.*

In spite of mutual suspicions, the members of

the two congresses were made to understand each other; they closed by uniting in the city which M. Rouher called *the city of lakes.* There, Gustave Chaudey, the future victim of robbers some of whom sketched there with him the plans of perpetual peace, called the vote of congress of Lausanne, and proposed aloud from the rostrum a compact in virtue of which the workingmen should aid the *bourgeois* in recovering political liberty, while the *bourgeoisie* in return should coöperate in the economic enfranchisement of the proletariat.

The congress of peace closed, amidst the roars of laughter of all Europe, by a grand mêlée and a Homeric exchange of International cuffs.

However, in spite of these blows with the fist, or, perhaps, thanks to them, a reconciliation was effected between the *bourgeois* demagogy and the laboring demagogy, and if we may believe M. Fribourg, it was in virtue of this alliance that the International took part in two revolutionary manifestations, which took place about six weeks later, one November 2nd, at the tomb of Manin, in the Montmartre cemetery, and the other the next day but one on the boulevard Montmartre to protest against the occupation of Rome by the French troops.

M. Fribourg deceives himself if he supposes that his friends and he could have prevented the mass of their army from taking part in these tumults; by opposing them, they would only have lost all their authority over them; it is always the application of the famous saying: as they were its leaders they had to follow.

The deputies of the Seine, although a large part of their electors belonged to these two division of the revolutionary party, abstained from going to what M. Fribourg calls "the rendezvous given by the militant democracy." Their absence excited deep indignation in the ranks of the manifestants.

The members of the International drew up a sort of *ultimatum* for these honorable deputies, whom they pretended to make their puppets, and summoned them to hand in their resignation, in order, they said, to enable the Paris electors to express themselves energetically against the Roman question.

The deputies had sufficient respect for themselves and their constituents not to obey this insolent and absurd summons, and doubtless more than one of the leaders of the demagogic party who publicly expressed astonishment at them, desired at the bottom of their hearts this independence which was forbidden to themselves.

The organizers of the association had been led, in spite of themselves, to declare war against the empire. The government decided to take up the gauntlet. The houses of some of the leaders were searched, but at none of them were proofs found of their participation in political intrigues or conspiracies. They ceased then to treat the International as a secret society, and contented themselves with prosecuting the members of the committee of the Paris bureau, as having belonged to an unauthorized society.

The accused were fifteen in number: Chemalé

(Félix-Eugène), aged twenty-nine years, architect; Tolain (Henri-Louis), thirty-nine years, chiseller; Héligon (Jean-Pierre), thirty-four years, printer of paper hangings; Camélinat (Rémy-Zéphyrin), twenty-seven years, worker in bronze; Murat (André-Pierre), thirty-five years, engineer; Perrachon (Joseph-Etienne), worker in bronze; Fournaise (Joseph), forty years, maker of mathematical instruments; Gauthier (Pierre-Michel), forty-one years, jeweler; Dauthier (Orésime-Irénée), thirty years, saddler; Bellamy (Jean-Victor), thirty-five years, turner; Gérardin (François-Eugène), forty years, house-painter; Bastien (Jean-Pierre), forty-five years, corset-maker; Guyard (Victor-François), thirty-eight years, worker in bronze; Delahaye (Pierre-Louis), forty-eight years, machinist; Delorme (Jean), thirty-six years, shoemaker.

The trial, brought before the sixteenth chamber, occupied two audiences, those of March 6th and 20th, 1868. The greatest precautions were taken in these proceedings, and although there were found in the private papers of the accused members, sinister threats against those functionaries of whom they thought they had reason to complain,* there were reserved for the enemies of social order

* "As for the note books, regulations, statutes which you sent me, I have received none of them. Vandal, without doubt, would have acted in this matter, for it is beyond the functions of the minister. We will have our revenge. Vandal, you may be sure we will not forget you." (Extract from a letter of one named Lécluze to Chemalé, one of the accused; extract quoted in the prosecutor's speech.)

some considerations which there was a reluctance to use against writers suspected of preferring a moderate republic or a constitutional monarchy to the empire. The imperial advocate commenced by declaring, in the most insinuating of introductions, that "his word, always impartial, would this time have to make no effort to remain calm, I was about to say kindly," towards the accused. Tolain defended his comrades and himself with a certain moderation. The tribunal, presided over by the celebrated M. Delesvaux, showed itself as "kindly" as the prosecutor, and, while declaring the "International association of workingmen established under the name of the bureau of Paris" dissolved, he contented himself with imposing on each of the accused a fine of 100 *francs*.

This sentence, excepted to by the condemned, was confirmed April 22d by the imperial court, after a long speech by Murat, who himself presented his defense and that of his comrades. Their petition in appeal was rejected November 12th.

The association had waited neither the sentence of the Supreme court, nor that of the Imperial court, nor even the primary judgment, to assume the part of treating as a dead letter the absolutely certain condemnation which awaited it. From Mar. 8th, a second committee was nominated, in which, says M. Fribourg, "the members were constrained to introduce a very strong party of *liberal Communists*," and which "it believed would emphasize the political tendency of the Paris workingmen."

We do not know in what respect the Communists

of whom M. Fribourg speaks were *liberal;* still it is true that it was not long before they in their turn became objects of the public prosecution. May 22d, M. Delesvaux saw the second committee come before him, about two months after he had condemned the first.

The accused were nine in number. They were Varlin, Malon, Humbert, Granjon, Bourdon, Charbonneau, Combault, Landrin, and Mollin. Like their predecessors, they continued to defend themselves, only they did it with much more violence, and declared themselves loudly, republicans and Communists. It was Varlin who played in the second trial before the police magistrate the rôle which Tolain played in the first; only he showed himself as passionate and as revolutionary as the defender of the association in the first affair had shown himself calm and sensible. M. Fribourg says that the International believed itself under the necessity of giving pledges to the political Jacobins. It seems to us that it submitted in all simplicity to the fatal law which invincibly carries away demagogism; the influence having escaped from the moderate party, the most violent and most crazy inherited it. Each of the nine accused was condemned not only to a simple fine, but to three months of imprisonment.

"Imprisonment strikes the second group," says M. Fribourg on this subject, "and places in daily contact the pseudo-Communists of the International and the Blanquistes of the affair of *La Renaissance.* What follows, may be easily conjectured;

deprived of their liberty, stigmatized *political men* by their condemnation, the prisoners lent an ear to the suggestions of the conservative party which, poisoning the minds of the workingmen, assured itself of more auxiliaries."

Some months later, the general council, speaking of the two trials in its report to the congress of Brussels, congratulates itself upon the effect which they had produced: "The governmental chicaneries," it wrote, "far from killing the International, have given it a new scope by cutting short the injurious coquetries of the empire with the laboring class."

However, it is lawful to question if its satisfaction was very sincere.

What is certain, is that the first condemnation frightened a certain number of its members. A letter, quoted in the prosecutor's speech at the time of the second trial, shows the real effect which it had produced upon these. A brave engraver, named Mathon, wrote to Chemalé, March 25th, a little ashamed and excusing himself much, that he and a certain number of his friends should abstain from going to a reunion appointed for the morrow. He adds very frankly and not in sentences which he would recall, that he will no longer be liable to a fine merely, but to imprisonment:

"We have not the means for passing six months in prison, because our children must live in our absence. As you see, and we are frank, it is not so much loss of liberty as need of work which hinders us and compels us to remain at home.

Besides, we think we have done our duty as honest men and devoted members, by signing the protest of March 6th, against the proceedings directed against the committee which compromised us almost as much as the committee itself.

"When one has seen 1848 and its retaliations, then 1852, one has fewer illusions!

"The International is dissolved, and well dissolved, as for the present, while waiting for other circumstances more favorable or other societies which can last.

"One last word in conclusion: do not believe that this is indifference or cowardice; it is reason which speaks, and necessity for work. Accept our thanks for the zeal and intelligence of which you have given proof as member of our committee."

III. THE FRENCH BRANCH DISGUISES ITSELF IN FEDERATION WITH WORKINGMEN'S SOCIETIES.—HATRED OF THE LEADERS OF THE ASSOCIATION AGAINST THE BOURGEOIS REPUBLICANS.—THEY ABUSE AND USE THEM.—HOPE OF A SPEEDY TRIUMPH.

"The International is dissolved and well dissolved!" That was a sentence which it was fully determined not to accept. They did not ask themselves for one moment if it were necessary to be annihilated, they only cared to seek means of legally dissembling its existence. There were a large number of workingmen's societies of all kinds, societies of resistance, syndicates, etc.;

which were either authorized or at least tolerated. It was resolved to bind them by means of a *Federal Chamber* and thus to organize a federation which would be nothing else, in reality, than the International itself with all its organization and all its means of action.

The administration could the less ignore this movement, as for its accomplishment it was necessary to hold a large number of reunions, almost all very numerous, which it was impossible to hold without previous authority. An account of strikes was given there ; funds for maintaining them were received there ; nothing, in a word, distinguished a federal assembly from an International assembly. The government decided to forbid these reunions during the month of September, 1869.

Immediately the society made haste to protest against these fetters laid upon liberty. The signers of the protest declared themselves decided to continue by all the means in their power the discussion of the scheme of laws of their federation.

One of the most constant customs of the leaders of the association at this time, was to present to the public and the *Corps législatif* all their claims by the journals, which at the same time they tried to kill, and by the deputies of the extreme left, for whom they boasted to profess the most supreme disdain.

The protest of which we have just spoken, had been inserted in *Le Siècle* of September 12th, 1869. At the same time, *Le Travail*, a journal published by the friends of the International, persuaded all the democrats to abstain from entering the coffee houses, ale-houses, taverns, and restaurants which had the audacity to persist in receiving *Le Siècle*, put under the ban of democracy. On December 25th of the same year, Varlin wrote to Aubry:

"*Le Siècle* is perhaps also at Rouen the journal of wine-merchants and tavern-keepers. You may organize against it the campaign which has been organized at Paris, of which you have read some passages in *Le Travail*.

"It is necessary to fight our enemies by every means possible, and, at the point where we are now, our most serious enemies are the moderate republicans, the liberals of all kinds."

Nothing is more curious than the profound contempt which they manifested in their private letters for all the great men of the party of *irreconcilables*, whom they obliged to defend themselves in public, and whom they overwhelmed with humiliations in private.

February 2d, 1870, Bastelica, writing from Marseilles to Varlin, tells him how it happened that MM. Gambetta and Esquiros addressed interpellations to the government concerning the strikes of Creuzot: "You are doubtless ignorant that Gambetta and Esquiros have interpellated upon our demand." The submission of which these heroes of implacable opposition gave proof, made the citizen Bastelica shrug his shoulders, adding in a tone of pity: "Our radicals are declining, declining. The low tide of public opinion is going very soon to leave bare the dilapidated keels of these old ships."

The day in which the leaders of the International saw these *old ships* floated again upon the waves by a revolution, their fury no longer knew bounds. Dupont wrote from London, September 7th, to Albert Richard, at Lyons :

"The piteous end of the imperial Soulouque brings into our power the Favres, the Gambettas. Nothing is changed, and the power is always with the *bourgeoisie*. In these circumstances the rôle of the workingmen, or rather their duty, is to let this *bourgeois vermin* make good peace with the Prussians."

This hate was not secret; the initiated made no effort to conceal it from all eyes ; they continued, on the contrary, to proclaim their disdain for the journals by which they had defended themselves and for the deputy puppets of which they pulled the strings. Thus, January 8th, 1869, on the eve of the general elections, Varlin wrote to Aubry : "We will enter into the electoral lists in competition with the *bourgeois* republicans of all shades in order to affirm the division of the people from the *bourgeoisie*."

The International acted, however, with the republicans of the secret societies and the barricades, as with the parliamentary faction of the *irreconcilables* ; it despised them ; it did not conceal it from them, and at the same time it used them. It is thus that Malon wrote to Combault, who went to Cosne, to recommend himself to Gambon ; at at the same time, he thanked him for having "purged the International from the calumnies of the *Blanquistes.*" In the trial of 1870, the imperial advocate had said that Blanqui, Tridon and Miot had attended the meetings of the congress at Brussels. This assertion seemed to Theisz, not only compromising from a judicial point of view, but injurious from a political point of view; he points it out with a certain sharpness: "That," says he, "does not concern us more than what precedes; but in the interest of truth, I must say that those citizens, whom we have reason to believe moderately sympathetic with the International, are not members of it; that only one came two or three times to the section of Brussels, that the others never placed their feet there."

At this time when, in spite of the trials and condemnations which it had undergone at Paris, the International was making everywhere, even in France, enormous progress, its chiefs had arrived at the conclusion that they no longer had need of the support of any party, that the association would be in a few years, perhaps in a few months, strong enough to throw down by itself alone all which had opposed its triumph, to stifle all who would resist it, that its victory would be so irresistible that it would be accomplished without contest.

This idea recurs in every form during the last two years of the empire, in the speeches of its orators, in the writings of the publicists:

"The International," we read in a speech pronounced at the congress of Basle (1868), "is and ought to be a state among states; it permits them to march on their way, until our state shall be stronger. Then, upon their ruins, we will place ours all ready, all made, such as exists in each section; *stand out of the way when I begin*, that will be the word." (Account given of the congress of Basle, page 7.)

Hear now how *L'Internationale* speaks, in its number of May 2nd, 1869:

"Revolution demands preparation; now when this preparation, which consists in the elaboration of a common programme of social renovation and in the grouping of the proletaries of all countries, shall be made, no outbreak will be necessary to work the revolution; it will be done easily, by the unanimous agreement of all proletaries, that is to say, of the population. And if then some lofty barons of capital and their likes in the *bourgeoisie* wish to oppose the social transformation, will not the proletariat stifle the barkings of these dogs in its powerful grasp, its huge embrace?"

This programme is also that which the general council displayed at the same time on the occasion of the events at Seraing, in the manifesto which we have quoted already.*

Sometimes it is well said that circumstances cannot, strictly, move as easily as one thinks, and that the old society will perhaps have the bad taste not to let itself be devoured with a good grace; but they were not afraid of this resistance, and they charitably advised the *bourgeoisie* not to attempt it.

It is thus, that an amiable correspondent of the

---

* See page 166.

International from Lyons, Madame or Mademoiselle or rather the citizen Virginie Barbet writes :

" As for civil war, we neither wish it nor provoke it ; nevertheless, we do not hesitate to declare with our usual frankness, that in order to avoid it, we no longer wish to make those cowardly compromises which complicate matters instead of clearing them up ;—if we are called to see the horrors of civil war, it is not because the laboring class has desired it, but the property class ; let these last yield to the first summons of those whom they have so shamefully speculated on, let them wisely consent to make them restitution justly demanded, and this grand social transformation will be accomplished without having to record much to be regretted acts."

The organ of the association in Austria, the *Volkstimme,* expresses these same ideas, in a shorter and more striking way : " For us," it says, " the red flag is the symbol of universal human love. Let our enemies take care not to transform it against themselves into the flag of terror."

IV. LAST MONTHS OF THE EMPIRE.—MINISTRY OF JANUARY 2ND.—FUNERAL OF VICTOR NOIR.—M. ROCHEFORT ; HISTORY OF THE " MARSEILLAISE." STRIKE OF CREUZOT.—CLUSERET ANNOUNCES THE INTENTION OF BURNING PARIS.—THE INTERNATIONAL BEGINS TO FEAR THE ORLEANIST PRINCES.

Such were the feelings of the members of the International at the beginning of the last year, at the time when the authoritative régime established by the *coup d'état* fell to pieces under the discontent and mistrust of the middle classes, and when some men well-meaning, but too feeble in character, endeavored to substitute for the dictatorship a constitutional government which would draw its power from the union of all moderate parties reconciled with the empire by freedom.

This generous and wise endeavor, it will be remembered, was pervaded from its commencement by a series of crises some of which led to dangers which no wisdom could have foreseen or averted, of which others were caused as much by the faults of the ministers as by those of their enemies. The events which determined these excessive crises were, it will be sufficiently remembered, the murder and burial of Victor Noir, the strike of Creuzot, the arrest of Rochefort, the agitation caused by the plébiscite, the affair of the Orsini bombs, finally, the candidature of the Prince of Hohenzollern to the throne of Spain, and the declaration of war which it determined. We must confess that nothing was more fitting than such shocks, to favor at the same time as the desires of the enemies of the empire, those of the enemies of society.

The first of these events, which no one could have foreseen, surprised the International and the Jacobin party as thoroughly as the government; but contrary to what ordinarily happens in France in the days of popular excitement, the government showed more skill on the defensive than its enemies displayed on the offensive. The letters seized on the principal leaders of the association, and quoted in the third trial, prove clearly that the revolutionary party, uncertain, divided, although it had had, between the death of Noir and his funeral, several days to assume its part, remained all day without plan and without direction, no more being able to decide to profit by so magnificent an occasion of disorder than to submit to letting it escape.

"The delegates of the federal chamber," (says Varlin in a letter addressed to Aubry, January 19th,) "were neither united nor concerted at first; all met with the majority of the members of the workingmen's societies at the burial of Noir; I can assure you that the larger part of them were disposed to act if Rochefort had said: *To Paris!*

"Rochefort was master of the situation. He was intelligent and reasonable enough not to give a fatal order and send to death the best soldiers of the revolution.

"It is he alone whom we ought to thank for the issue of that day. As for the people, if they did not take the offensive themselves, it was because at first they lacked arms, and because, besides, they understood that the strategic position was the worst possible."

While Varlin praised Rochefort thus, Bastelica at Marseilles condemned him without hesitation: "Rochefort is culpable," (he wrote to Varlin;) "I am severe, but just. One must not play like that at sliding in the blood of the people." According to the citizen Bastelica, the hero of the Faubourgs of Paris is already in February a played-out man:

"Why does not Rochefort resign? That man, (whom I hold in high esteem,) has had, like men who serve the revolution, his day, his hour, his latitude. To-day the popular level has gone beyond him; let him regain the shore, if he does not wish to be drowned. Let us have another!"

Demagogism breaks quickly its toys!

And, moreover, there was a very convenient toy which this *vaudevilliste* mislaid in politics. What an admirable puppet for the International which pulled the strings, as Malon explains to a workingman of Saint-Etienne. "*La Marseillaise*," says he, "is a revolutionary socialist journal which is quite at our disposal, and which will insert with eagerness all the communications which the International will send to it."

Varlin, in a letter to Aubry, lets us privately into the secret of the foundation of *La Marseillaise*. *Le Travail* had just died. The socialist party wished for a long time to have a journal for itself, so as to be no longer reduced to defend itself through the journals of the *bourgeois* republic. But they could not succeed in obtaining the necessary capital, when Rochefort was nominated deputy to Paris:

"With its own resources," (says Varlin,) it is evident that the socialist party could not have created an organ, but with Rochefort the difficulty was removed, not by his fortune, for he has none, but by his name.

"A journal started by Rochefort is assured of success. In France, the crowd attaches itself before all to that which glitters, and as assurance of success gives confidence to capital, Rochefort has found lenders. The financial question being settled, the rest became easy.

"The most devout socialists, and especially the members of the workingmen's societies, met at a private reunion and discussed the conditions upon which they would establish the journal. Millière, nominated manager, was at the same time and especially charged with the socialist line of the journal.

"This line is the one affirmed by almost all the delegates of the International at the congress of Basle, that is to say, the collectivist socialism or indiscriminative Communism."

Poor Rochefort! When he wrote his amusing "*Mystères de l'hôtel des ventes*," when he played his gay songs "*L'Homme du Sud*," and "*La Vieillesse de Brididi*," who could then have foreseen that we would one day see him descend to parading the mountebanks of Communism, and becoming the file-leader of demagogism!

The International, which had its journal, *La Marseillaise*, since the end of 1869, was not less taken unawares the day of the funeral of Victor Noir; it understood that it must not expose itself to being found a second time in grave circumstances without unity of plan. The search for practical means to arrive rapidly at a mutual understanding and a union in view of the same action, was the order of the day of all the federations; they were occupied with it as busily at Marseilles and Lyons as at

Paris, and it seemed that the problem had been solved, inasmuch as twice, September 4th and October 31st, the disasters of the country served as a pretext for a display of shields on the part of the demagogy, which took place, with the most perfect uniformity, in most of our large cities.

In the month of February, 1870, France was not yet sick enough ; the ravens of the International did not consider the time as having come for alighting upon it ; they held themselves aloof from outbreaks which gave occasion to arrests. While the Jacobins, *bourgeois* Republicans, were barricading the *boulevard du Temple*, and Flourens was making his famous expedition for the conquest of wooden swords and tin pistols at the theatre of Belleville, Varlin, Malon, and Combault issued a proclamation signed in their names, in which the violence of the style only served to render acceptable to the impatient ones the pacific determination which they decided to take—" What is most important," they said, " is to assure the success of the revolution ; and being conscious of our strength, we are concentrating it. The cup is full. It will not be slow in overflowing. Let the revolution choose its hour."

During this time, the excitement that the crime of Auteuil had caused in all the ranks of the population was maintained and increased in the laboring class by the strikes which were organized almost everywhere.

The most famous of those which broke out at this time was that of Creuzot, which was excited by a man then unknown, whose name to-day has become too celebrated, the machinist Assi. What was the real motive of the strike? Did the International, which had everywhere for some time urged the workingmen to free their treasuries of assistance from the direction or the surveillance of employers, especially covet the rich treasury of Creuzot? Must we believe what it said then, and see in Assi the voluntary or unconscious instrument of a political intrigue hatched in the ranks of the Bonapartist party which had just been overturned by the ministry of January 2nd? That is only a supposition, and no proof has up to this time been given to sustain it. What is certain is, that whatever was the motive of Assi, this strike and its furious declamations, for which it served as the pretext, indisposed the popular masses against the director of Creuzot, and did at least as much evil to the politician as to the great manufacturer. But at the very same time that they wounded M. Schneider personally, they were to contribute to throw discredit through him upon the chief of one of the grand departments of state, and, indirectly, on the assembly even over which he presided; they inflamed the passions already so ardent of the laboring classes against the empire and the *bourgeoisie*.

The leaders of the extreme opposition rendered an account sufficiently exact of the considerable results which they had produced in shaking all the foundations of the empire at once. All saw that the edifice of December 2nd ran the risk of falling at the very moment when it received its crowning-stone. Only, while the least intelligent believed that the fall of the imperial monarchy would only be profitable to socialism, the more far-sighted began to see that the Bonapartes once overturned, another enemy more serious would be able to dispute their spoils with the conquerors.

A former officer, turned out of the French army on account of facts of a nature to sully his honor, the *soi-disant* General Cluseret, had made at Sainte-Pélagie, where he found himself in the character of a political prisoner, the acquaintance of members of the second committee of the International.* He had felt there a serious power; he had seen men determined to succeed and little scrupulous as to the choice of allies who could help them in throwing down society; he joined himself to them, calculating to succeed by their aid, determined to do everything to succeed, as not to draw back from any crime in order to maintain himself when he should be in power, or to avenge the day in which he should see himself defeated.

As soon as he was out of prison, as by having himself naturalized as American citizen he had lost the title and rights of a French citizen, the government hastened to request him to leave France. He returned to America, this time on account of the International. He thought for a moment of founding a journal for preaching the doctrines

* "I send you inclosed a programme (for a journal) which Cluseret, our fellow-prisoner at Sainte-Pélagie, seized for us. He did it upon the demand which was addressed to him by an important trade interest." (Letter from Varlin to Aubry, January 8th, 1869, quoted in the third trial.)

pronounced orthodox in the congress of the asso-cition, and particularly for recruiting members.

On learning in the month of February, the events at Paris and the troubles for which the death of Victor Noir and the arrest of Rochefort had furnished the pretext, he renounced his project, considering that it was no longer the time for words but for action.

A letter which he addressed from New York to Varlin, bearing the date of February 17th, 1870, is worthy of being quoted entire, for it proves that this man, doubtless a stranger to the passions and prejudices which blinded the other members of the International, and driven to join them by ambition alone, was singularly clear-sighted; it proves at the same time that all the crimes of which he was afterwards guilty, had been for a long time premeditated, and that he had resolved for a long time not to perish without dragging down Paris in his fall:

NEW YORK, FEBRUARY 17.

MY DEAR VARLIN:

I have just received your good letter of the 2nd. It explains to me the delay occasioned to the solution of my question: it is needless to tell you that I accept, and that I am going to throw myself into the work of endeavoring to be useful to my brothers in misery and labor.

The journal of which I spoke to you is not founded, and I do not think it my duty to renew the attempt in view of the late events in France, which as well as the letters of my friends, unanimously call me back to Europe.

According to all probability, I shall be there by next summer; but, by that time, I shall have organized the International relations between the various French and American groups, and have designated to take my place (subject to the choice of the French committee) one or more persons zealous and capable.

As you say, we will triumph surely, infallibly, if we persist in demanding success for the organization.

But let us not lose from sight that the organization has for its end the uniting of the largest number for action.

Then let us be smooth, let us round off the angles, let us be really brothers in action, not in word ; let the words of doctrine and of individuality not separate us from those whom a common wrong, that is to say, a common interest, has united ; we are everything and all ; it must be confessed that if we are beaten, we deserve it.

I have not seen that we have figured in the late troubles. What has been the attitude of the workingmen's societies and what are their actual dispositions ?

Certainly we must not sacrifice our ideas to politics, but it will be disastrous if we detach ourselves from them even momentarily.

To me, all which has just occurred signifies that the Orleanists are gradually making their way into power, cutting the nails of L. N. so as only to have to substitute themselves for him some fine morning.

Now, on that day we ought to be ready physically and morally. *On that day, we or nothing!* Until then I will probably remain quiet ; but *on that day*, I promise you, and I always mean what I say, *Paris will be ours, or Paris will be no more.* That will be rhe decisive moment for the accession of the people.

Yours, CL——*

"On that day, we or nothing! On that day, Paris will be ours, or Paris will be no more!" Events have proved that this was not sinister boasting, but a project maturely settled. Other facts, also revealed to the public, unfortunately incredulous, by the imperial advocate in his prosecution of June 22nd, 1870,—eleven months before the burning of Paris—will furnish at need additional proofs.

At the house of one of the members of the In-

---

* This curious letter was quoted in the prosecution of the imperial advocate, during the third trial.

ternational, a private dictionary was found, which gave the key to their ciphered correspondence, The proper or common names which they used most frequently, were translated each by a particular sign. Now, we find among these current words of their language not only *arms*, *powder*, *ammunition*, but also *nitro-glycerine* and *picrate of potash.* If we do not meet with the word *petroleum*, it is doubtless solely because the Prussians had not yet at this time taught these grand citizens the surest method of burning our cities.

At the house of one of them, Pindy, whom we found to our misfortune this year at Paris, there were seized some things still more compromising than this private dictionary enriched by such terms. They had discovered the recipe for the making of nitro-glycerine, that of a composition of carbonate of sulphur, and that of a powder of chlorate prussiate of potash. Some of these recipes were followed by this direction : " To be thrown into windows ; " others with this note : " To be thrown on the eaves."

Pindy, when pleading his own cause, pretended that if he had copied these alarming indications, it was solely to satisfy a sentiment of curiosity. "The accusation made of me," said he, " a dangerous man, and if the tribunal drew logical conclusions from the words of the imperial advocate, I shall be sent to Cayenne. And, nevertheless, it is very difficult to find in me the character of a fierce conspirator, dreaming only of pillage and assassination. Assuredly I recognized that, for the need of the accusation, it was well to reproduce against the International some of the formulas; the subversive passions, the unwholesome doctrinces, the barbarous and savage engines, in a word, all the accessories which serve to frighten and to excite against socialism all the Joseph Prudhommes of the *bourgeoisie.*" Alas! Joseph Prudhomme was not sufficiently frightened March 18th; he paid dear in the month of May for his excessive confidence!

The passage relative to the contingency of the destruction of Paris was not, without doubt, in the the letter of Cluseret, that which had the most news for Varlin. He was to be much more struck by this idea that the revolution which had advanced might well, upon the whole, profit not only the socialists, who would have the trouble of causing it, but the Orleanist princes who would hold themselves aloof from it. This letter, written February 17th, should have reached him in the first part of March. The 8th of the same month, that is to say, probably three or four days after he received it, he wrote to Aubry:

"You are wrong in believing for one moment that I neglect the socialist movement for the political movement. No, it is only from a truly socialist view that I pursue the revolutionary work, but you must well understand that we can do nothing, in the way of social reform, if the old political state is not annihilated. We do not forget that at this time the empire only exists in name and that the government is the injury of parties. If, in such grave circumstances, the socialist party lets itself be rocked to sleep by the abstract theory of sociologic science, we may well wake up some fine morning under new masters, more dangerous for us than those whom we overthrow at this time, because they will be younger, and consequently, more vigorous and more powerful."

In Paris, as in New York, after the beginning of the year 1870, more than four months before the declaration of war, six months before the fall of the empire the men most implacable against the social order trembled at the idea that the princes of Orleans, if they arrived at power, would have the force which was wanting to Bonaparte, that they would and that they could protect effectually all that the International had promised itself to throw down.

V. THE PLEBISCITE. — AFFAIR OF THE BOMBS. — THIRD TRIAL OF THE INTERNATIONAL.

Meanwhile, the ministry of January 2d had committed the fault of deciding to urge a plébiscite on the occasion of the excellent reforms which it was preparing to have voted by the senate. It will still be remembered, even after the terrible events which it brought about, the agitation which this decision, unfortunate and impolitic from every point of view, spread through the country.

The International could not fail to profit by it. After the 11th of April, the federal section of the French branch published a very short address, dated at London, which closed thus: "We can vote neither for the parliamentary empire nor the arbitrary empire. We will all vote for the republic by casting blank ballots in the urn. No abstaining. Blank ballots."

It is known that immediately the word of command was changed, and that all the revolutionists, to whatever division of party they belonged, commenced an active propagandizing to increase, by all possible means, the number of *No's*, which decided many liberals to vote *Yes*, in spite of their repugnance to the empire.

The plébiscite was as much the pretext and as much the motive of a number of public reunions, called often by the members of the International speaking officially in its name, and still oftener by the leaders of the association, but without official character.

Most of these reunions began by conferring the honorary presidency upon a fanatic of the Jacobin party, named Mégy, who had just made hmiself dear to the demagogues, by shooting with a pistol the agent Mourot, charged to arrest him. Some gave themselves as many as three honorary presidents at once; then the name of Mégy appeared preceded or followed by those of Garibaldi and Rochefort. It was in one of these assemblies, where were gathered fifteen hundred or two thousand workingmen, that the contract of federation of the Paris workingmen's societies was voted. A committee was also nominated there, charged with preparing a plan of an anti-plebiscitary manifesto in the name of the International. Combault and Johannard were on it.

"Our speculators divided the rôles," says Varlin at this reunion, "to-day all must be changed.

Already the International has conquered the prejudices of the people as a people. We know to whom we owe it, under Providence, who has always inclined to the side of the millions; the good God has taken His time. Enough of this. We appeal to those who suffer and who resist. We have the power and the right; we must suffice for ourselves. It is against the judicial, economic, and religious order that we must direct our efforts."

Combault shows himself still more violent:

"Never," he cried, "has the laboring class been willing to accept anything whatever from the conqueror of France, whom it has always regarded as its most cruel enemy. The International has submitted to the hard laws of necessity; it was killing itself up to the time when it could say: We do not wish the empire; and for several years it is its sharpest cry. We must occupy ourselves with politics, since labor is submissive to politics. We must say aloud, once for all, that we desire the social republic with all its consequences."

The ministry of January 2nd could not tolerate such attacks. M. Emile Ollivier commanded all the attorney-generals to watch the International closely, and arrest its leaders.

"Has the International at Marseilles been seized?" (he wrote, for example, to the attorney-general of Aix). "It certainly exists there. I am told that the reunions at Marseilles are intolerable because of their violence. Do not hesitate to make an example, and especially strike at the head."

At the same time, they closely watched the group of republican Jacobins, great friends, as it is known, of conspiracies and strong admirers of Armodius and Aristogiton. It was then that was discovered, a few days only before the opening of the ballot for the plébiscite, the famous plot of the bombs, and that the *Journal officiel* published the report of M. Grandperret, attorney-general, to the minister of justice, upon the intrigues and projects of the revolutionists.

All shades of the republican party were unanimous in declaring that the conspiracy was an invention of the police, an electoral manoeuvre hatched by the government itself, desirous of frightening the electors so as to prevent them from voting against it. Such a position is no longer tenable to-day, at least unless one is willing to admit that the 18th of March itself and the Commune of Paris were also inventions of the police. For the men denounced by M. Grandperret, and afterwards tried before the supreme court of Blois, were precisely all those heroes of March 18th and of the Commune who did not belong to the International, such as Villeneuve, Flourens, Guérin, Fontaine, Tony Moilin, Mégy, Cournet, Tridon, Rigault, Jaclard, etc.

But it is true that the International took no part in the affair of the bombs, and its language conformed at the same time to the truth of the facts and to its secret thoughts when it issued, May 5th, the following protest:

"The Paris federal council of the International association of workingmen presents a formal contradiction to the accusations and insinuations of the official and officious journals.

"It is false that the International had anything to do with the new conspiracy, which doubtless, had no more reality than the preceding inventions of the same order.

"The International knows too well that the suffering of all kinds which the proletariat endures, belong much more to the actual economic state than to the accidental despotism of a few makers of *coups d'État*, to lose its time in dreaming of the suppression of one of them.

"The International association of workingmen, a permanent conspiracy against all oppressors and all speculators, will exist in spite of all the powerless prosecutions against the *soi-disant* leaders, as long as all the speculators, capitalists, priests, and political adventurers shall not have disappeared.

"For the Federal Council, the members present: Ansel, Berthemieu, Bertin, Boyer, Chaillou, Chalain, Chaudey, Cirode, Combault, Dambrun, Delacour, Dupont, Durand, Durieux, Duval, Fournaise, Franke,* Franquin, Giot, Haake, Langevin, Malézieux, Mongold, Marlet, Ménard, Pagnerre, Portalier, Reynier, Rivière, Robin, Rochat.

"MAY, 2ND, 1870."

This manifesto was a declaration of war not only against the men of the empire, clearly designated by these words, *political adventurers;* but also against the *bourgeoisie*, the clergy, and every man who had any interest whatever in the maintenance of social order.

No one outside of the International itself was surprised or scandalized to learn that the leaders of this famous society were for the third time the object of judicial prosecutions.

This third trial, which occupied several long sittings, would have deserved to have excited the public to the highest point of interest, by the

* This name is written thus in the journal from which we take this document. Is it not a mis-print, and should it not rather read *Frankel?*

authentic and innumerable documents seized at the houses of the accused, in which the real plans, the private hopes of the partisans of social overthrow were revealed in the most complete manner. The reading of an excellent prosecutor's speech, in which the history of the association was skilfully and patiently written, not with hypotheses and hyperboles, but with certain facts, with the letters of the accused themselves, occupied all the hearing of June 22nd.

On the 29th, the imperial advocate abandoning the general ground, which it had held at the privious hearing, approached the question of law which had become involved in the trial, and sought to establish that, if the International concealed neither its existence nor the names of its members, nor the place and time of its reunions, it none the less fell under the stroke of the law against secret societies, because, behind the patent end which it published, it followed another more mysterious, which it concealed with care. This argument, more ingenious than solid, was developed with skill, but it seems to us difficult and dangerous to admit it. Finally, the speaker reached the charges which weighed in particular upon each of the thirty-eight accused. They were divided by the accusation into two categories, equal in number: the first nineteen were accused of having, during less than three years, taken part at Paris in a secret society, as chiefs or founders; the other nineteen were accused of having been simple members.

It is indispensable to reproduce here these two

lists; in fact, the larger part of the names of the central committee and of the Commune will be found here.

The accused of the first series were: MM. Louis-Eugène Varlin, aged thirty-one years, binder; Benoist Malon, twenty-eight years, bookseller's-assistant; André-Pierre Murat, thirty-seven years, machinist; Jules Johannard, twenty-seven years, foliage-maker; Louis-Jean Pindy, thirty years, joiner; Amédée-Benjamin Combault, thirty-two years, jeweller; Jean-Pierre Héligon, thirty-six years, book-broker; Augustin Avrial, twenty-nine years, engineer; Pierre Sabourdy, thirty-six years, employed on the journal *La Marseillaise;* Jules Colmia, called Franquin, thirty-two years, lithographer; Auguste-Jules Passedouet, thirty-two years, journalist; Marie-Antoine Rocher, thirty-six years, publicist; Adolphe-Alphonse Assi, twenty-nine years, machinist; Camille-Pierre Langevin, twenty-seven years, metal-turner; Félix Pagnerre, forty-six years, foliage-maker; Charles Louis-Paul Robin, thirty-three years, teacher; Albert-Félix Leblanc, twenty-six years, civil engineer; Paul-Jean Carle, thirty-two years, teacher; Camille-Félix Allard, twenty years, law-student.

The nineteen others are: MM. Albert Theisz, thirty-one years, chiseller; Adolphe Collot, thirty-two years, joiner; Eugène-François-Germain Casse, thirty-two years, journalist; Jean-Désiré Ducauquie, thirty years, weigher; Emile-Amour Flahaut, thirty-three years, marble-cutter; Bernard Landeck, thirty-eight years, jeweller; Louis Chalain, twenty-five years, copper-turner; Bernard-Gabriel Ansel, twenty-nine years, painter on porcelain; Frédéric Bertin, thirty-two years, iron-moulder; Vincent Boyer, twenty-nine years, stone-cutter; Barthélemy Cirode, thirty-two years, sculptor; Alphonse Delacour, thirty years, binder; Gustave-Emile Durand, thirty-five years, jeweller; Emile-Victor Duval, twenty-nine years, iron-founder; Joseph Fournaise, forty-two years, maker of mathematical instruments; Léo Frankel, twenty-six years, jeweller; Giot, twenty-one years, painter; Malzieux, forty-two years, blacksmith.

By adding to the list of the thirty-eight accused of the third trial of the International that of the accused who appeared, some days later, at Blois, before the supreme court of justice, to answer concerning the Jacobin plot of the Orsini bombs, there will be had nearly a complete list of the members of the central committee of the national guard and of those of the Commune of Paris.

The revolution of March 18th, was arranged and operated conjointly by the Internationals and the *bourgeois* republicans. We have already said several times what sentiments of distrust and aversion these two revolutionary parties nourished with respect to each other. It is easy then to understand the violent hatreds which divided the ephemeral masters of the *Hôtel de ville,* and which would not permit them long to hold power, when even Flourens, Duval, and Bergeret himself would have succeeded in seizing upon Versailles and dispersing the "rustics."

A large number of the facts which we have exposed in the course of this book, and the documents upon which we rested in order to justify our assertions, are, as have been seen, borrowed from this trial, which is up to the present time with the official accounts rendered of the congress, the richest and surest source from which the historians of the International should draw. We could only repeat what we have already said elsewhere, if we wished to follow step by step the inquiries and the defense of each accused. We will limit ourselves then to giving the result of the trial by saying that Assi, Ducaucquie, Flahaut, and Landeck were acquitted, because it was not "sufficiently proved" that they belonged to the International: that Varlin, Malon, Murat, Johannard, Pindy, Combault, and Héligon, proved guilty of having belonged to a secret society, were condemned to one year's imprisonment and a hundred *francs* fine; finally, that all the others were acquitted of being leaders of a secret society, but being considered as having belonged to an unauthorized association of more than twenty persons, they were condemned to two month's imprisonment and a fine of twenty-five *francs*.

We have said that this trial should have attracted the attention of the public; unfortunately, minds were turned in another direction; very few readers took the trouble to run over in their journals with absent eyes the very summary accounts given of the first hearings; as for the last, at the time when the journals gave the analysis of them, the candidature of the Prince of Hohenzollern for the throne of Spain had just been revealed; the question of a war between Prussia and France was agitated, and closed the mind to any other political anxiety.

No one suspected, July 9th, 1870, that the obscure names of these workingmen, condemned as members of a secret society or unauthorized association, would be very soon connected with the most horrible disasters of France, and that these men, whom the police magistrate had just condemned to light penalties, would appear at the end of a year before the councils of war after having led pillage, murder, incendiarism for two months and a half through terrified Paris.

CHAPTER X.

THE INTERNATIONAL AND THE WAR.

I. THE INTERNATIONAL CONDEMNS NATIONAL WARS.—IT ONLY ADMITS SOCIAL WARS.

Of all the questions which the International approached in its general or federal congresses, or in its official or officious organs, that upon which it varied the least, that which is always solved in the same way, from the first day to the end of its doctrine, and to the most extreme consequences of its principles, was the question of war.

It condemned war at the same time in theory and in practice; it wished to deprive governments of the means of making it, by destroying the standing armies, and when it sought to prove to us the urgent necessity of a social revolution, conducted simultaneously in all the European states, the argument on which it insisted most vigorously, was that the actual governments could not live without armies, and that the armies which they possessed, led them fatally to make war against each other.

The theory which the fathers of the new demagogic church displayed a hundred times in their speeches or in their writings, can be summed up nearly in this way:

The causes of wars in the actual state of Europe are of two principal kinds: the one belongs to the *economic anarchy*, the other to the personal ambition of the sovereigns and the princes, to the selfish interests of the governing class.

The consequences of every war are at least as disastrous to the conqueror as to the conquered, for the people which triumphs loses generally a part of its liberties because its rulers profit by the éclat and the power which their victories give them, either by restricting the liberties already existing or by delaying concessions which they would have been obliged to make.

The "workingmen" especially, upon whom war presses more heavily than on the other classes, both by the augmentation of taxes of all kinds which it causes, and by the increase of the tax of blood, payed almost exclusively by them, never have any chance of withdrawing from these sanguinary contests, of which the profit goes to the privileged classes.

Even among the conquerors, the workingmen suffer directly and indirectly from the best conducted and most happily terminated war, while they receive no kind of profit from the most brilliant victories.

Even among the conquered (we are giving always the theory of the International,) the *bourgeois* classes profit by the most unfortunate war. In fact, they gain this at least, that political questions, placed in the fore-ground, drive off for a little time the study and solution of social problems; moreover, the defeat of their country, by renewing national hatreds ready to die out, render more difficult the understanding between the workingmen of all Europe, without which social revolution is almost impossible.

Such is the résumé as faithful and exact as we can make it, of the doctrines displayed at all times and under all forms in the journals and reunions of the International.

By the side of many errors and illusions, this theory contains, it seems to us, a sufficiently strong element of truth.

The Crimean war, by permitting Napoleon III to establish more firmly his despotism, by virtue of the prestige by which it held its power, gained by a night's attempt, retarded for ten years the awakening of liberal ideas in France.

The conquered Russians have, on the contrary, owed to their defeat political reforms of great importance and the prompt construction of their network of railroads.

Vanquished in 1859 at Magenta and at Solferino, Austria found itself thrown by its defeat into the course of most useful reforms, while the victorious emperor of the French only made some feeble accessions to liberal ideas, and, maintaining the reality of his absolute power, continued to see in liberty only a simple "article of exportation," according to the fortunate expression of Prévost-Paradol.

France, crushed in 1870 and 1871 by the armies of all Germany, gained at least by its defeat the fall of the malefactors who stole the power in the dark night of December 2nd, and recovered the free disposition of itself. The victorious Germans became by the very fact of their victory the humble subjects of Prussia, and lost in liberty and autonomy more than they gained in prestige.

It is beyond a doubt that the wars which we have just recalled in no way profited the laboring classes of the countries which bore off great victories, and that the Germans, especially, lost by the triumph of the Germanic Cæsar all hope of being employed for a long time in our workshops, in our magazines and our bureaus, where they found positions at the same time more agreeable and more lucrative than those which the Prussian conquerors can offer them to-day.

It is evident that we have not taken sides, and that we render justice to the International itself when we can discover in the torrents of error and madness which it has poured forth over the world, some just and wise ideas.

But we must not exaggerate praise. The International endeavored less to prevent war than to change its place.

Up to the present time nations have hated and fought against nations, while recommending concord and mutual affection to the children of the same country.

The International changes all this. It no longer recognizes the distinctions of nationalities; "labor," it says, "has no boundaries;" but it excites the workingmen of all countries to hate, combat, plunder, and oppress those whom they call *bourgeois, capitalists, speculators, monopolists, parasites,* that is to say, the classes which live not by manual labor, but by intellectual labor, or by the fruits saved from any labor whatever. It abolishes national wars, but only to replace them by social wars.

The general council of London by no means conceals it, and in its manifesto concerning the *civil war in France,* it says without circumlocution that the only war which can be justified in all history, is that of the enslaved against their enslavers.*

It was in order to more easily gain the victory in this war that the International, and with it all the divisions of the demagogic party, so energetically claimed the suppression of standing armies, which were guilty of impeding the realization of their plans of social regeneration, and of retarding the "return of landed property to social collectivity."

The congress of Geneva, in 1866, approved a report decisive in its condemnation of standing armies, the general arming of the people, and its instruction in the use of arms.

In 1867, the congress of Lausanne decided unanimously "to adhere fully and entirely to the congress of peace, to sustain it energetically, and participate in all that it may undertake in order to realize the abolition of standing armies and the maintenance of peace, so as to arrive as soon as possible at the emancipation of the working class and its deliverance from the power and influence of capital, as

---

* . . . in the war of the enslaved against their enslavers, the only justifiable war in history.—(*The Civil War in France, p.* 31.)

well as the formation of a confederation of free states of all Europe."

The congress of Brussels finally debated at length the same question of peace and war, and sought a practical means which would permit "workingmen" to render wars impossible henceforward.

M. De Paepe, of Brussels, proposed two means: the first was "the refusal of military service, or," added he, "what amounts to the same thing, since the armies must necessarily be consumers, the refusal of labor." The second was, "to solve the social question itself," that is to say, to accomplish European social revolution. "This is," he added, "the method which the continual development of the International will make triumph."

Another orator, also Belgian, named Spehl, proposed "exciting against war the conspiracy of the whole working people."

The congress in its last sitting, listened to the reading of a plan of resolutions presented by Becker, "in the name of the group of the section of the German language," which, in the midst of the the customary invectives against the *military*, the *ruling classes*, etc., contained this prophetic sentence:

"Considering that every European war, and especially a war between France and Germany, should be regarded to-day as a civil war, *profitable at most to Russia,* whose social state is not yet at the height of modern civilization."

However, the resolutions adopted at "administrative meetings," that is to say, in private sessions, were not those of the group of the German language, but nearly those which the French group presented, by the organ of M. Tolain. The congress protested against war "with the greatest energy," invited all the sections of the association to act "with the greatest activity" in their respective countries, so as to prevent "a war of people with people, which to-day can only be considered as a civil war." Finally, adding to the ideas of Tolain the hardly practical plan of De Paepe, it recommended to the *workingmen* "to cease all work in case war should break out in their respective countries;" and it finished by urging all *workingmen* to sustain "this war of the nations against war."

II. PROTEST OF THE INTERNATIONAL AGAINST THE WAR OF 1870.

Such were the dispositions of the adherents of the International, when the conflict between France and Prussia supervened.

Three days before war was declared, *Le Réveil*, in its number of July 12th, published a manifesto of the Paris members of the association "to the workingmen of all countries."

Very just ideas were mingled in it with inevitable invectives and commonplaces.

"In response," we read, "to the warlike acclamaations of those who are exempt from the tax of blood or who find in public misfortunes a source of new speculations, we protest, we who desire peace, labor and liberty. War is the indirect means of governments for stifling public liberty."

The signers addressed themselves particularly to their *brothers in Germany*, to urge them not to listen to "the mercenary or servile voices which should seek to deceive them concerning the true spirit of France," and to their *brothers in Spain*, to recommend to them not to let themselves be transported by the conquests of their more recent revolution.

This address bore a very considerable number of signatures. We notice among others those of MM. Tolain, Murat, Avrial, Pindy, Theisz, Fournaise, Avoine Junior, Camelinat, Varlin, Langevin, Johannard, Assi, Mégy, Bertin, Cyrille, Rousseau, Delaunay, Levy, Dupont, Pothier, Chalain, etc,. who some months later were to sit in the *Hôtel de ville* as members either of the central committee, or of the Commune. During the days following, a large number of the sections of the International sent their adhesion to this manifesto.

July 23nd, the general council addressing, in its turn, "the members of the International Association of Workingmen of Europe and the United States," related after its fashion, the history of France during twenty years, and that of Prussia during ten years. It stigmatized with the same energy "Louis Bonaparte" and "Bismark" and in the midst of much violence, abuse, and calumny, hit upon some words and ideas truly just in their brutality:

"The plot of war of July, 1870, is only a new *coup d'Etat* of December, 1851, revised and corrected. Whatever may be the issue of this war, the funeral knell of the second empire has already sounded in Paris. On the side of Germany the war is defensive, but who is it who has put Germany to the necessity of defending itself? It is Bismark who has conspired with Louis Bonaparte in the aim of stifling popular opposition at home, in the interior, and to take away Germany from the dynasty of the Hohenzollerns. If instead of having been gained, the battle of Sadowa had been lost, the French battalions would have overflowed Germany as allies of Prussia. After the victory, did Prussia think one moment of opposing free Germany to enslaved France? Quite the contrary. The Bonaparte régime, which had only flourished until then on side of the Rhine, has to-day its counterpart on the other. In that state of things, what could result except war?"

The authors of this manifesto lacked neither memory nor perspicacity:

"If the working classes of Germany permit the actual war to lose its strictly defensive character, and to degenerate into an offensive war against the French people, a victory or a defeat will be equally disastrous, all the miseries which desolated Germany after its war for independence will be revived with increased intensity."

The grand council then recalled several manitoes voted by different German sections of the International, in response to the address of the French workingmen. Some of these quotations are wise invitations to concord. Others, on the contrary, are only an appeal to social war. Thus, at Chemnitz, the general council tells us, a reunion of delegates representing 50,000 Saxon workingmen, after having declared that according to its view, the war which had just broken out was purely dynastic, adds; "We will never forget that the workingmen of all countries are our friends, and the despots of all nations our enemies."

According to the International the *despots* are all those men who do not gain their support by manual labor; we must not forget this in judging of the true meaning of this phrase.

After the first series of our disasters and the fall of the empire, a movement of sympathy in favor of republican France appeared in the sections of the International, not only in England, but also in Germany.

We will not quote in support of this fact all the official documents which we find in the journals of the association. But we are bound at least to make known a manifesto very honorable for the socialist party beyond the Rhine, which was published in the duchy of Brunswick, at Wolfenbüttel, as soon as the revolution of September 4th, was learned there:

"As long," it says, "as the armies of Napoleon threatened Germany, it was our duty, as Germans, to push to the end the war of defense, the war in the name of the independence of Germany. But in presence of a victory so glorious, it is more than ever our duty not to be intoxicated by it, but to ask ourselves calmly what we have to do. The actual democratic government (that of Paris) will be penetrated with the feeling that the French and German peoples are brothers, which have the same interests, the same duty of uniting in the spirit of modern times, to vie with each other in the arts of peace. It will seek to free France from the enemy by peace. But it is necessary that this peace be made easy for it, that is to say, an honorable peace must be offered to them. It is in the interest of Germany to conclude an honorable peace with France, for a disgraceful peace will be only a truce which will last until the time when France shall feel herself strong enough to shake off the disgrace. It belongs to the German workingmen to declare that, in the interest of France and Germany, they have decided not to tolerate an injury done to the French people, after it has freed itself for ever from the infamous person who disturbed the peace. It is in the name of the socialist democratic party of workingmen, that we protest against the annexation of Alsace and Lorraine. And we are responsible for all the German workingmen. The German workingmen, in the interest of France and of Germany, of peace and of liberty, in the interest of Western civilization as opposed to Cossack barbarism, will not suffer the annexation of the French provinces."

The authors of this declaration went so far as to quote a saying, as hard as just, from a letter of one of their friends in London: "As Germany commenced by only finding its unity in the Prussian barracks, it is a chastisement which it has well merited." But as it must be, in all which emanates from the International, that the best things (when by chance we find some good in such documents) are spoiled and destroyed by the most deplorable ideas, this very sage manifesto concludes with a cry in favor of "the International contest of the proletariat;" now we have established by numerous proofs that the contest preached and dreamed by the association whose history we are tracing, is only and can only be the most violent and most implacable of social wars.

As soon as this document appeared, General Vogel von Falkenstein arrested the members of the workingmen's democratic socialist committee, and sent them chained to the railroad which transported them to Koenigsberg. Such is at least the account which we find in *L'Egalité* of September 22nd, 1870, with the signature of the two most celebrated chiefs of the socialist party beyond the Rhine, MM. Bebel and Liebknecht.

We will not extend farther these quotations from manifestoes which the war, whose first act had just closed, gave birth to in almost all the sections of the International. It remains for us to see how the French members of the association conducted themselves in the midst of these terrible events.

CHAPTER XI.

THE INTERNATIONAL AND THE REVOLUTIONS.

THE 4TH OF SEPTEMBER AT PARIS AND IN THE PROVINCES.—THE SIEGE OF PARIS.—THE CAPITULATION.—DISORGANIZATION OF THE SOUND PARTY OF THE NATIONAL GUARD OF PARIS.—ORGANIZATION OF THE CENTRAL COMMITTEE.—THE 18TH OF MARCH.

We have seen that the German members of the International while protesting against the war of 1870, recognized boldly the necessity of defending German territory against the aggression of France. They only condemned it, in an absolute manner, when it had changed its character and become on the part of Prussia, a war of conquest. Still their protest had no other effect than to cause the arrest of those who had written it, and we have never heard that a single soldier of the regular army or of the militia, deserted or refused to fight in order to remain faithful to the theories of the association concerning wars between nations.

It was not the same with us, and the French members of the International only showed courage and resolution for civil war.

We regret not to be able any longer, in this last part of our work, to corroborate our assertions as we have constantly done, up to this time, by official proofs, by unimpeachable evidences. It is a too recent history; the documents which will serve to write it are still in the hands of the councils of war and the examining magistrates. We shall hope, however, that faith will be given to our assertions, because they all relate to facts for which public notoriety can, up to a certain point, replace written proofs.

Every one remembers the stupor and indignation which was excited everywhere in France by the announcement of our first disasters, of that frightful day of August 6th, in which we lost two great battles.

The first cry of every Frenchman was then for arms. Each one swore to himself to brave every peril in order to repulse the enemy who defiled by his presence the sacred soil of the country.

In the midst of this general enthusiasm, the demagogic party was distinguished by its ardor in claiming guns; but it was not against the foreigner that it proposed to turn them. One might already guess its sinister projects on the day when the wretches assassinated the firemen of *La Villette*. We do not forget that on that day, almost at the very place where the crime was committed, a reunion of the International was to have been held, which was forbidden at the last moment, and that the members of the association, who had come to this rendezvous, blocked up the street at the time when the post of firemen was attacked.* Let us

* A writer devoted to the cause of demagogism, Madame André Léo, addressed to different Paris journals, some days after this assassination, a letter in which, conforming to the traditions of her

not forget, also, that one of the assassins, Eudes, condemned to death for his participation in this crime, and set at liberty some days later, September 4th, as a political culprit, was, after the 18th of March, one of the generals of the Commune.

---

party, she accused the police of having slaughtered the unfortunate firemen of *La Villette* in order to accuse the International of their death. Do not the facts which she relates turn against her clients? The reader shall decide for himself. We let Madame André Léo speak for herself:

"Last Sunday, a reunion of the International was to have taken place in the *Rue de Flandres* at two o'clock, (which generally means three.) The threats of the commissary of police to the doorkeeper of the hall prevented this reunion at the last moment, so that a large number of persons who had come to attend it, found themselves at from three to four o'clock on the boulevard at the end of the *Rue de Flandres*. They were peaceable groups. They conversed upon public misfortunes. Upcn what other subject could they speak?

"I left that point at half past three, a little before the event, which I learned only in the evening from several friends. They experienced, like myself, a dolorous stupefaction. They had been witnesses of it, since *our people at that hour filled up the boulevard. This coincidence struck us;* we thought that they wished to compromise the International. Who? We did not know; but we remembered the saying, Whom will the event profit?

"Monday we read in *Le Petit Moniteur:* 'The leader of the attack seemed to be one named Périn, one of the leaders of the International.' The International has no leaders, and Périn by no means figures in the list of the arrested.

"And now *La Gazette des Tribunaux* tells us of the existence of daggers said to belong to the International, giving thus the appearance of a verified fact to an infamous invention. The International has no daggers. It did not take part in the attack of *La Villette*. It believed only to have recognized there Guérin escaped from Blois."

We borrow this letter from *L'Egalité* of Geneva, August 27th, 1870.

On the evening of Saturday, September 3rd, we learned of the disaster of Sedan. On the morrow, at the same hour, Lyons, Marseilles, Toulouse, and Paris proclaimed the republic. The cockneys were in ecstacy over the simultaneity of these movements, and found in that the proof that they were entirely spontaneous. We are permitted to recall to the men who reasoned thus, that after the affair of the funeral of Victor Noir failed, Varlin and Bastelica exchanged letters in which they spoke of the necessity of an organization, of an understanding which henceforward would, in grave circumstances, make their friends obedient in all France to one and the same word of command. It is lawful to believe that the understanding was established during the few months which separated the drama of Auteuil from the tragedy of Sedan.

At Paris, it is true, the chiefs of the International had only seized, on the 4th of September, positions relatively secondary; committees of all kinds, (of surveillance, of vigilance, of equipment, etc.,) established in the town halls, commands in the National Guard, etc. We have already quoted ourselves the letter in which Dupont complained so bitterly to Varlin of seeing "the Jules Favres, the Gambettas" in power, and advised letting *this bourgeois vermin* ruin itself in signing the shameful peace which Prussia imposed upon us. However, it must be remarked, that if the notoriety of the deputies of the extreme left had in some manner imposed them at Paris as members of the provisional government, the power had fallen at Marseilles and Lyons into the hands of the lowest demagogism.

The *Commune,* which had been installed at Lyons, commenced by assuming the red flag, which is, as we know, the flag of the International. At Marseilles it had been the same, and if the prefect nominated by the municipal provisional committee, M. Labadié, belonged no more to the association than M. Challemel-Lacour, the prefect sent to Lyons by the government of the national defense, these two functionaries of the new power were none the less ruled by a crowd of vagabonds who imposed on them all their wishes. We know what rôle the *civic guards* played at Marseilles, and the *clubbists* of the *Rotonde* at Lyons; now the violent measures which these men, the scum of the population of the two cities, undertook and executed themselves, or which they imposed upon M. Challemal-Lacour and M. Esquiros, belonged nearly all to those who had extolled for two years the publicists and the orators of the International.

The *federation of the Communes,* decreed at Lyons by the statesmen of the *Rotonde,* is the basis of the political organization claimed by the association. The *Ligue du Midi,* which made so much noise in the departments of the basin of the Mediterranean, was, with some variations, nearly the same thing as this famous federation. The partisans of the *federation* and the adherents of the *Ligue du Midi* signalized themselves by vying with each other in their hatred against regular armies, as in their zeal in arresting the generals and lavishing on them the worst treatment and insults. Both armed with strength the men who were enrolled under their red rag ; neither the one nor the other ever led them against the Prussians ; both thrust them later into civil war ; both, finally, tried to utilize the services of the famous citizen General Cluseret, the grand tactician of the International, and both, thank God, were successively defeated in all their battles. But if we cannot yet, for want of sufficient information concerning facts and persons, establish what is the respective part of each division of the demagogic party in the troubles of the Rhone and the mouths of the Rhone, it is nevertheless clear that the men and the ideas of the International played a great rôle there.*

At Paris, one could guess in the first part of the the siege what was the plan of the too famous association. Its friends and bribed orators spoke no longer of the suppression of the frontiers and seemed animated, with respect to the Prussians, with sentiments analogous to those which we all experienced. We could even, if our memories do not deceive us, number several of them among the partisans of war to the utmost and of a sortie *en masse.* But what was especially remarkable, was the order with which the battalions, devoted to the cause of social revolution, laid in stores of chassepots and cartridges.

It was permitted to believe that these intrepid

* The successor of of M. Labadié to the prefecture of Marseilles, M. Delpech, a book-keeper September 4th, and general in the month of November, thanks to M. Gambetta, was a member of the International.

warriors were going to cause terrible moments to the subjects of the king of Prussia. However, when the battalions on the march were sent to the out-posts, it was perceived that they were those of the most International *arrondissements* who applied themselves with the most zeal to "falling back in good order" or even to flying in disorder at the first attack, at the first alarm, and General Clément Thomas pointed out this instructive fact to the leaders of the *Journal officiel.*

On the other hand, throughout the entire siege, the persons engaged in the revolutionary manifestations and the *coup-de-main* attempts, belonged almost exclusively to the Jacobin party; the International refrained *en masse* as well October 31st as January 22nd.

What then were they doing? They were holding themselves in reserve, wishing neither to expose their precious welfare against the Prussians, nor to exhaust themselves in useless skirmishes against power, nor to foolishly take possession of the *Hôtel de ville* just in order to have the shame of opening the gates of famished Paris to the enemy. While waiting, they recruited, counted, organized, and increased each day of waiting their stores of cartridges—without mentioning those who, in the artillery of the National Guard, studied in their leisure moments the art of loading cannon and maneouvering the *mitrailleuse.*

At last famished Paris was obliged to capitulate, and the Parisians were able to go out of the walls, within which they had been shut up for four months and a half. The most of those who profited by this permission were the *bourgeois* in a hurry to see again their property in the provinces, or to protect interests more or less gravely compromised by the interruption of communications between the departments and the Capitol. These were the leaders of the trade, the men of leisure, the capitalists, the men of order. A large number wore the epaulettes of officers or the lace of subalterns in the National Guard; their prolonged absence more or less completely disorganized the battalions of the central quarters. During this time, those of the outer quarters no longer fearing the Prussian balls, organized in view of the social war. The federation of the battalions of disorder was accomplished with little noise on the plan of the federation of the workingmen's societies. The National Guard commenced by possessing, without doubt, a *central committee* which was increased each day by some of the celebrities of the International.

When the day fixed for the entrance of some Prussian regiments into a quarter of Paris arrived, the occasion was deemed favorable by the chiefs of the association, struck with the confusion of what remained of the government at Paris. We do not need to record here how the cannon scattered through different parts of the city were all at once carried off by the trust-worthy members of the central committee, under pretense of preventing them from falling into the hands of the enemy, and conducted to the culminating points of the outer *arrondissements* gained over to the cause of social revolution. We will not describe those eighteen days of moral disorder and intellectual anarchy during which the government, disconcerted and disorganized, let the scum of the Paris population drown the unfortunates suspected of having belonged to the police, and plant the red flag on the summit of the column of July.

One morning, this agony of the regular powers was terminated by the defeat of the attempt made to retake the cannon of Montmartre. On that day the central committee inaugurated its bloody power by the assassination of the Generals Lecomte and Clément Thomas.

At last the International triumphed ; happily, its reign was short.

We have only to recall here the picture of these bloody orgies and the criminal insanities which terrified Europe. Everyone knows them, and the end which we proposed to ourselves is not to repeat once more this history already written so often, although the day in which it can be usefully written is not yet come. We have only wished to show by what series of mad ideas, by what impulse of disordered passions, the men who associated themselves, seven years ago, to accomplish by strikes the rise of wages, were led at first to believe that the empire of the world would belong to them, then to pollute themselves by the most appalling crimes on the day when they saw their chimeras vanish before the mournful reality of defeat and chastisement.

Our work would be finished if it did not remain for us to prove that not only the International is really responsible for all the crimes of the Commune of Paris, but also that it accepts, or rather claims, this responsibility as a title of honor.

CHAPTER XII.

THE INTERNATIONAL SINCE THE FALL OF THE COMMUNE.

During the last hours of the terrible conflict which gave Paris back to France, when we learned the news of the first fires lighted by the soldiers of the Commune beating a retreat, the journals of the demagogic party in the provinces remaining faithful to the word of command given by the Commune itself, apropos of the powder explosion on the avenue Rapp, commenced to accuse the *Versaillais* of having themselves fired our houses and our palaces, in order to blast the memory of the vanquished, to whom would be imputed such a crime.

It was difficult to sustain this system to the end, and to pretend that M. Thiers had also assassinated the hostages in order to increase the public indignation against the innocents to whom it would impute the massacre.

Everyone supposed that the political friends of the men who had disappeared in these waves of blood and smoke, would endeavor either to unburden, by we know not what falsehoods, their memories of these crimes, or to disavow them entirely and leave to them alone the entire responsibility of such guilt.

We saw very soon that we were mistaken. The flames were still rising from the ruins of the *Hôtel de Ville*, when already in all Europe many sections of the International, and the largest number of its journals, publicly proclaimed their admiration and gratitude towards the incendiaries.

At Zurich, June 4th, a reunion of members of the International of that city declared, unanimously, that "the combat sustained by the Commune of Paris is just and worthy, that it is in keeping with the ideas of a better time to come, and that all men who reflect ought to fight with it."

At Brussels, the Belgian section of the International, in a reunion held June 5th, adopted, also unanimously, a protest against the intention announced by M. Dumortier, of delivering up as malefactors under common law, the assassins and incendiaries of Paris. Here is the complete and authentic text of this protest. Too much publicity cannot be given to such an act, for it is the best means of branding its authors:

"Considering that M. Dumortier has thought fit, in the sitting of the chamber of the 25th of this month, to instigate an extreme and extra-legal measure against the defenders of the principles proclaimed by the Commune of Paris;

"That, in an intention evidently provoking and injurious as regards the Belgians who shared the views and approved the proceedings of the Commune of Paris, the said Dumortier has compared these glorious defenders of liberty and of human and common rights, to assassins, to robbers; in a word, to men beyond common law and not worthy of being considered as citizens;

"Whereas, the acts accomplished by the Commune of Paris, from its advent to the last day in which it could sustain itself, have been acts eminently political and social, having for their end either to destroy pre-existing wrongs or to inaugurate the era of justice in political and social organization;

"Whereas, if, in order to destroy these wrongs and make right prevail, the Commune of Paris resorted to force, it was because the eternal adversaries of right and justice had themselves brought the contest upon the ground of force, and that, nevertheless, after fruitless steps taken at different times with the assailing power, no one doubts that force alone would have obliged the reaction to yield before the just claims of the Commune of Paris;

"Considering that, in these circumstances, it is clear that the assassins were not on the side of those who defended the right, principles, justice, and liberty, but on the side of those who did not hesitate to employ the most infamous and most extreme means for stifling forever the attempts at vindication;

"The congress of the International Association of Workingmen protests in the most energetic manner against the calumnious imputations and malignant incitements emanating from M. Dumortier; solemnly proclaims the Commune of Paris vanquished for the time; recognizes that it has merited well of all mankind, and that those who have fought for it have right to the respect and the sympathies of all high-minded men."

At Geneva, two days before the entrance of the troops of Versailles into Paris, a reunion of the International voted an address to the Commune of Paris, in which it declared that this assembly expressed "the economic aspirations of the working classes," and that "when the workingmen are united by an organization as vast as that of the International, the triumph of their cause is assured."

Paris once retaken, the organ of the men who had voted this address, *L'Egalité*, did not conceal the admiration which the crimes by which its friends had crowned their work, caused it. This journal praises "the people," who by burning our palaces, have "destroyed the monuments of barbarism and the tabernacles of monarchial prostitution."

Here also quotations, rather long, are necessary to show by what a fit of mad rage the demagogic party was seized, when it saw the victory, which it thought it already held, escape from it:

"At the time when our brothers and sisters are perishing in the midst of the flames, forced to defend themselves against the brigands of Versailles and to keep their promise to bury themselves under the ruins of their liberty rather than let themselves be assassinated by the *Chouans*; at the time when those who are the dearest to us in the world are perishing, those who were the pioneers of our great work, those who will forever leave an irreparable void in our International family, we have not the heart to amuse ourselves with combatting the infamies of the reactionary press; the future reserves for us another combat.

"As for ourselves, let us utter one single wish: that this conflagration may at last illumine the people of the provinces; that this conflagration may kindle vengeance in the heart of the people, vengeance against the miserable brigands who could only save their monarchical order by forcing the people to burn themselves under the rubbish of the martyred city."

The same journal is still more violent in its number of June 10th.

"Our enemies can threaten us with surrender into the hands of the hangmen of Versailles, with expulsion from all corners of the civilized world, with a fierce pursuit against us all, who dare to proclaim our adhesion to the cause of the Commune, but our sympathies and our coöperation will not remain less active, and if the *civilized* world cannot tolerate us, let it then get rid of us by means of massacre and assassination, for in no way whatever, will we ever make peace with it, and if some more corpses *are necessary to the reign of order*, let them have these corpses, the *civilized* world will only fall more quickly.

"Massacre and persecute the working people, our association will no less persevere in its work of vindication, and will only lay down its arms when it shall have triumphed over your rascality.

"Let the Marquises of Gallifet ask our old men if they remember the days of June! We have the belief that those among us who shall survive their murders, will be still young and vigorous, when they shall say to them: We also remember the days of May, the massacres of men, women and child-dren, and we also recall the cry: Long live the Commune! Long live the International solidarity of workingmen and workingwomen!

"Foolish and impotent assassins of Versailles, what do you bring to France to make her forget your butcheries? Nothing but cannonades, destruction, transportations, dark conspiracies for the reës-tablishment of a monarchy, and in the distance the contest between imbecile pretenders, and new mas-sacres in the name of order,—the order of the grave. No, that is not what can *pacify* the world. The work of pacification was brought us by the Commune, the *Chouans* have hindered it from the first moment, they have barred the way to social reforms, by forcing all the population to occupy it-self only with military organization; no matter,—we knew what the Commune brought us, we have told it in our preceding numbers, and we will re-turn to it again and always until the definite tri-umph of the International revolution of working-men."

The German adherents of the International also declared themselves, in their journals and their re-unions, in complete community of ideas with their "brothers" of Paris. A socialist sheet published at Leipsic under the auspices of two members of the *Reichstag*, MM. Liebknecht and Bebel, did not hesitate to print the following: "We are and we declare ourselves to be in harmony with the Com-mune of Paris, and we are ready to sustain its acts at every moment and against everybody." M. Bebel himself, as we read in different journals, had just published a pamphlet in which he affirmed to the "workingmen of all nations" that the association is not crushed under the weight of the events at Paris, and that it has lost none of its means of action. At Barmen, a city of the circle of Dusseldorf, an assembly convoked by the democratic socialist committee saluted "the workingmen of Paris," as "the champions of the European proletariat," affirming that the cruelties for which they had been reproached had been made necessary in self-defense, and that the government of Versailles was alone responsible for them.

The Italian International played its part in this concert, and June 18th, a reunion of the Milanese sections, at which, it is said, 2,540 members of the association were present, voted an address which closed thus:

"To capital which said to them: You will die of hunger, they responded: we will live by our work.

"To despotism, they responded: We are free!

"To the cannon and the chassepots of the leagued Reactionists, they opposed their uncovered breasts.

"They fell, but fell like heroes.

"To-day, the reaction calls them bandits, places them under the ban of the human race.

"Shall we permit it? No!

"Workingmen! At the time when our brothers of Paris are vanquished, hunted like fallow deer, are falling by hundreds under the blows of their murderers, let us say to them: Come to us, we are here: our houses are opened to you, we will protect you, until the near day of revenge.

"Workingmen! The principles of the Commune of Paris are ours: we accept the responsibility of its acts.

"Long live the Social Republic!"

MALDINI, GIOVACHINI, DUPONT LÉON.

At London, the Internationals considered themselves not sufficiently numerous to testify in a public manifesto their adhesion to the crimes of their friends in Paris ; but in their private reunions they expressed their sympathy for the Paris Communists and their execration towards the troops of Versailles. One of them, as an English journal relates, even represented the " good time " as near. " Very soon," he said, " we can dethrone the English monarchy, convert the palace of Buckingham into a workshop, and throw down the column of the Duke of York, as the noble French people threw down the Vendôme column."

The burning of the Tuileries and the destruction of the Vendôme column particularly excited the admiration and stimulated the zeal of the Internationals of London. This is how an English journal recapitulates the speech pronounced by a Mr. Johnson in a meeting held at Sussex Hall, towards the middle of the month of June :

" The workingmen, who, since the fall of the Commune, have blushed for it, are to be blamed. The Commune had perfect right to have the hostages executed. The life of an archbishop is not worth an atom more than that of any other man. As for the destruction of the column of the Place Vendôme," the speaker adds, " I hope to put my own hand to the overthrow of certain monuments which are the disgrace of the west end of London. I would not destroy the palaces, no; but I would wish to convert them into lodgings for the poor. More than that, I would convert the churches into democratic and social clubs."

These lugubrious boastings were taken seriously by some English papers. Hear, for example, the *Evening Standard*:

"We ought not to be surprised to hear it said that henceforward London will be the center against which the attacks of the Socialist party will be directed. There is no army here to repress by brute force the apostles of the new religion. It is at London, we may reasonably expect it, that the vessel of the Commune, beaten by the waves, will find a port of refuge. The philosophers who contemplate with calmness the ruins of Paris will show themselves less easy when they see a committee of public welfare installed in Leicester Square. And who can say that this would be an impossible event? At the rate in which we are going in the way of social regeneration, we may yet live long enough to be witnesses of it."

All the quotations which we have made will suffice to show with the strongest evidence the true, secret thought of the International concerning the Commune of Paris, and the crimes by which its reign was opened and closed. However, it may be objected that such or such a section had not the right to pledge the entire association; that with much more reason the editors of *L'Egalité* are only responsible for what they print in their journal, and that we cannot without supreme injustice render a whole society of several millions of members responsible for speeches made in the meetings by a few orators who are, after all, to use the celebrated saying of M. Rouher, only individuals without commission.

Unfortunately for the International, it cannot invoke arguments of this kind, for its legitimate representatives, the members of the general council of London, chosen, it is said, by the delegates of all the sections represented in the congress, thought that they ought to make known their official opinion in a joint utterance on the events at Paris.

Now they also admired the burning of the palaces, they justified the massacre of the hostages :

"The Paris of the workingmen, in the act of its own holocaust, has enveloped in its flames its monuments and its edifices, so that the conquerors who have rent the living body of the proletariat, can no longer hope to enter triumphantly into the untouched architecture of their own homes. If the acts of the workingmen of Paris have been those of vandalism, it was the vandalism of despair, and not that of triumph, not that which the Christians committed upon the priceless treasures of heathen antiquity.

"The true murderer of the Archbishop Darboy is M. Thiers. The Commune, many and many a time, offered to exchange the Archbishop and a number of priests into the bargain for Blanqui alone, who was in the hands of Thiers. Thiers obstinately refused."

This interminable statement, in which, in order to justify and glorify them, they took up, one by one, each of the thoughts, words, and deeds of the Commune, concludes by a veritable apotheosis of the men of March 18th :

"The Paris of the workingmen and its Commune will be forever regarded as the precursors of a new society. Its martyrs are placed upon the altar of the great heart of the working classes. History has already nailed its exterminators to that eternal pillory whence all the prayers of their priests will not succeed in bringing them down."

We must say, however, that some of the men who passed in the eyes of the public for the chiefs of the highest authority in the International, endeavored to free themselves from their responsibility, or even condemned the crimes glorified by their former friends.

We related in a preceding chapter what M. Tolain said on the platform of the National Assembly on the subject of Communist theories preached in its congresses. The sole fact of not having quitted the Assembly when his colleagues of the Paris deputation laid down their commissions was, nevertheless, a protest against the crimes of the association which counted him among its founders.

M. Fribourg, of whom we have also had occasion to speak several times, addressed on his side a letter to *Le Soir*, in which, not content with energetically condemning the crimes of the Commune, he explains, in his way, the march more and more criminal, of the International of which he was also one of the first members :

"MR. EDITOR :

"A feeling of reserve which your readers ought to appreciate, made us postpone the continuation of our work on the International.

"On the morrow of the terrible crisis which we have just passed, it seemed to us suitable to wait and observe "the truce of the parties."

"But since the minister of foreign affairs, in his circular to the diplomatic agents, seems to confound in one and the same reprobation all the members of the International, and as, through ignorance doubtless, he makes the founders of the association responsible for the crimes committed in Paris by a handful of wretches, the scum of all parties, our duty is to continue our recital.

"We hold to what is well known, that an honest mind has never been able to conceive the thought of giving birth to a society "of war and hatred," and that the history of the International is divided into two parts: to the first period, which we call Parisian, belong the formation and the two first congresses of Geneva, '66, and Lausanne, '67. During this time the association was *mutualist*, that is to say, demanding for collective action only the guaranty of execution of contracts freely discussed, freely agreed to.

"In the course of the trials begun by the empire, the moral direction escaped necessarily from the hands of the French workingmen, passed to Belgium, and in this second period, called Russo-German, the International became Communist, that is to say, despotic.

"From that time it was easy to foresee the march of events: the fatal invasion of all the dried-fruit of the world into the bosom of the International, the possibility of grouping all secret ambitions and the near advent of *Babouvism*.

"It is against all idea of complicity with that sect which they have always fought, that we protest in our character of founding members of the International, and while remaining deeply devoted to the emancipation of the proletariat, we have the right to cry out, recalling a saying of Proudhon: We wash our hands of all these vulgar lupercalia?

"FRIBOURG."

We have already in other chapters replied to the theory of M. Fribourg as to that of M. Tolain, and we believe we have proved, as we went along, that the march of the International in the way of the false and the odious was constant, and even perfectly regular; that it by no means resulted as these gentlemen believed from accident, from chance, from the proceedings directed against the first bureau of the committee of the Paris sections, but that it must have inevitably resulted from the composition of the society and the ideas already absolutely false and singularly disastrous which had inspired its first founders. We will not return to this subject, and we will content ourselves with giving here the speech of M. Tolain, and the letter of M. Fribourg.

Protests less clear than those of these two gentlemen have been produced recently in England.

The manifesto of the general council, of which we have just spoken, appeared with the signatures of all the members of that council and all the corresponding secretaries. Some time after it was made public, their appeared in the *Daily News* two letters, in which it was criticized and disavowed. What was curious about it was that the author of one of these two letters, Mr. Lucraft, was one of the signers of the manifesto. But he explained that he had not been present at the meeting in which it had been adopted and that his signature had been used without consulting him. The general secretary of the council, Mr. John Hales, answered with much warmth, bymeans of the same journal.

After having thrown out sufficiently mysterious insinuations against the first of these two claimants, Mr. Holyoake, he said that, in the meeting of May 23d,Mr. Lucraft was informed that the address on the civil war in France would be read in the next regular reunion of the council May 30th. He had then only to decide whether he would be present or not at this reunion. Moreover he knew (let us notice in pasing the important detail which is revealed to us by chance), that the rule of the council was to make all its members figure as signers of these public documents, without troubling itself as to whether they were present or absent, and Mr. Lucraft, far from condemning this rule, had energetically insisted, in other circumstances, in preventing its being violated. In this very sitting of May 23rd, he voluntarily declared that "his entire sympathy was with the Commune of Paris." Finally, in the sitting of June 20th, he had been forced to acknowledge that he had not even read the letter, against which he had protested, and as for what had led him to disavow it, it was simply what he had read about this affair in different papers.

Mr. Odger also condemned the manifesto, although his name also figured among those of the signers: he moreover declared like Mr. Lucraft that he had ceased to belong to the council.

Mr. Hales finished his letter to the *Daily News* by declaring that these two resignations were unanimously accepted.

New incidents were still produced in this affair of the disavowal of the address by some of its pretended authors, and new explanations, generally very confused, were published by means of the papers. We will not dwell upon them, and will only recall the two facts which seem to result from this curious incident.

The supreme leaders of the International evidently adhered freely, spontaneously, we have even the right to say passionately, to the doctrines of the Commune of Paris. They approved its deeds and its crimes ; they thought it useful to their cause to manifest, by a public document, this adhesion of their vast association ; then, seeing what profound disgust this abominable statement, in which they exalted the incendiaries and glorified the assassins, inspired in the immense majority of the public, several of them regretted having yielded to their first movement, and sought a means of separating themselves from a society, without doubt numerous and powerful, but henceforward doomed to general execration.

CONCLUSION.

REAL POWER OF THE INTERNATIONAL.—HOW CAN IT BE RESISTED? — LAWS OF COMPRESSION; THEY WILL DO MORE HARM THAN GOOD.—ORGANIZATION OF AN INTERNATIONAL RESISTANCE TO THE INTERNATIONAL CONSPIRACY OF DEMAGOGISM.

We have exposed as faithfully and clearly as we were able, the principles, organization, and deeds of the famous association which pretended to work immediately, in one day, by a single blow of irresistible power, the most profound and radical revolution which had up to this time overthrown Europe.

Now that we have shown the serious danger which threatens society, we will, perhaps, be asked to point out the remedy. That would be an attempt beyond our power; we will not venture to undertake it, but we will allow ourselves at least to present some observations by way of conclusion.

We believe first, that, however great may be the evil, the perils which it brings upon us must not be exaggerated.

In war, the power of the enemy does not result solely from the number of men which it places in line; this question of numbers is even relatively secondary. That which makes the power of an army, principally, is the character of the soldiers of which it is composed; it is especially the ability, intelligence, and science of the leaders who command it.

Now the soldiers of the International are not worth much. Those of the workingmen who are not content to adhere to the statutes of the society in order to free themselves from fatiguing importunities, to avoid being thought evil of by their comrades, but who embrace its principles with passion, and who count on their triumph as Moses counted on the promised land, are generally the least industrious, the least patient, the least economical, the least sober. The fanatics of the society, those who must constitute its principal power, are furnished not from the flower, but from the scum of the laboring class. Here is already a cause of weakness.

The leaders are perhaps supplied still worse. Those who were the most intelligent and the most honest among the first founders, are almost all disgusted and have retired. What are the others worth? We have seen them at work for our injury; what proof of talent or of intelligence have they given? When have they shown themselves capable of commanding? They are divided among themselves, and the noise of their discords has often drowned at certain times the noise of the cannonade; but they have not known how to organize their government nor even one of their battalions. They passed two months of their reign in undoing in the evening what they had done in the morning, and in making decrees which no one obeyed. The true formula of their government was *anarchy in despotism.* They obtained less submission with their committee of public safety, their court-martials, and their vollies of musketry, than the most common-place of ordinary governments obtains with the three-cornered hat of an inoffensive policeman. That which ought to humiliate them the most, if they took note of it, was that the sentiment which they inspired in most unanimously in everybody, and first in their own friends, was contempt. And this contempt was precisely because of their profound ignorance of all matters, and their incurable incapacity which pervaded every one of their actions. Here, truly, were generals capable of conquering the world!

A socialist school recognized the necessity of the union of three elements in every enterprise: labor, capital, and talent. The International is recruited, especially, among the *workingmen* little friendly to work: it declares capital infamous, and smites it with excommunication; as for talent, it has shown that its leaders were completely destitute of it. It may still, perhaps, give us some bloody fight, but we have little reason to fear that it can ever, in whatever part of the globe it may be, win a serious and lasting victory.

However, if we need not fear seeing it triumph, it is certain that we must guard against the evil which it can and which it will do us.

What ought we do to in order to resist it?

The means which at first seems the most simple, is to have recourse as ever to repression. God forbid that we should be led into this course so easy in appearance, so fatal in reality. Withdrawal of the law of coalitions and reëstablishment of the articles of the code which condemned strikes, absolute proscription of the right of meeting, and the right of association, severe laws against the press, such are the sole barriers which people to-day think of opposing to the progress of the enemies of social order. Alas! we have already set up against them these pretended barriers: they have singularly restricted the movements of honest men, scrupulous observers of the laws, and prevented them from doing good; they have not arrested for one moment the others, who care little for law and have little fear of prison.

On the one side, some have abstained, out of respect for the law, from holding meetings in which serious questions relative to arts, commerce, and trade would have been usefully discussed; on the other side, some have known well how, in contempt of the law, to hold secret conventicles in which war against society was organized.

The law hindered us from associating in order to reclaim, under the second empire, the large liberties and prudent reforms which might have prevented our late disasters; it did not hinder the founders of the International from uniting by hundreds of thousands in their association, men determined to risk everything in order to establish the reign of Communism.

The organic decree of February 17th, 1852, subjected the political press to the control of the primary authorities and administrative jurisdiction, under pretense that it was the sole means of saving society when in danger. The functionaries of the empire applied this law of safety with marvellous intelligence. Leaving on the field of the discussions of the press all the fundamental principles on which society reposes, they reserved warnings and suspensions for the journals guilty of vexing prefects or disturbing ministers. Certain statesmen of the second empire thought they were giving a proof of their political genius by protecting against the rigors of the tribunals the ultra-socialist sheet of M. Vermorel which preached social war, at the very time when they were forbidding honest liberal conservatives to start a paper which might bear an Orleanist tinge.

Such will be infallibly always and everywhere the effect of laws of compression. We have had since December 2nd a proof of it, too long, too sad, and too decisive, to allow us to care to try it over again.

It is then not the State which we must ask to protect us against the International; it is ourselves who must consider the means for defending ourselves all alone.

The country in which it has done the most evil is that which enjoyed almost no liberty at the time in which it was founded, that is to say, France. In the states where almost absolute liberty reigns, like Switzerland, Belgium, England, it has had to limit itself to organizing strikes which have often succeeded, but which have sometimes also failed.

Let us imitate the Belgians, the Swiss, and the

English. Let us fight error by opposing to it truth : but especially let us become organized for the contest.

The workingmen united in order to sustain each other in their strikes. Let the employers unite in order to resist these coalitions. The day in which they shall decide to sustain each other as energetically as the workingmen do, they will be the strongest. In England, since the leaders of industry have succeeded in opposing their coalitions to those of the workingmen by their look-outs, the strikes have become much less numerous. In Geneva last year, the employers in the building-trade adopted the same system, and stopped all their works, as soon as the strike of the plumbers, organized with great influence, broke out. Therefore the plumbers could no longer count on the subsidies which their comrades had promised them, since they needed aid themselves ; the plans of the ringleaders were disturbed; in spite of all the efforts of the International the strikers had to yield and return, discontented doubtless but beaten, to the workshops which they had hoped to reënter only as conquerers.

The association which attacks the employers is international. Let that which they shall form to defend themselves be international also. The day in which all the capitalists—since it is for them that it is desired—shall become associated from one end of Europe to the other in order to defend themselves, they will no longer yield before any coalition, and instead of dreading their defeat, it will only remain to us to exhort them not to abuse their victory.

The day in which they shall triumph, their first care ought to be to show themselves generous and benevolent towards the vanquished, the bitterness of whose defeat they should endeavor to make supportable. They ought especially to endeavor to make their workingmen understand that this war between labor and capital is more senseless than culpable, that the interests of these two pretended adversaries are identical, that the employer would be as crazy to seek to starve his workingmen as the workingmen to wish to ruin his employers, that the same qualities are necessary to one as to the other, that order, economy, activity, and intelligence, have often transformed a simple workingman into a *bourgeois*, a capitalist, as disorder, idleness, and prodigality, have often caused a family to fall from the ranks of the *bourgeoisie* into those of the proletaries.

It is true that these truths, and all those of the same kind, are hard to impress upon the minds prejudiced, and moreover, little enlightened and especially exasperated by a recent contest. But there must be joined to these philosophic and economic preachings, proofs clear and irrefutable of the benevolent and just spirit with which they are animated. There are many workingmen laborious, active, intelligent, to whom the claims made in advance in all strikes, by the leaders of the International, are very prejudicial because they tend to substitute work by the day, advantageous only to idle or unskillful workmen, for work by the job, favorable to the good and skillful laborer. In this choice number, from which already the *bourgeoisie* is recruited, will there not be means of finding a large number of honest men who can and who will wish to serve as loyal and respected intermediates between their comrades and their employers? Could there not thus be organized regular arbitrators who, standing aloof from either party, can make capital understand one day the just claims of labor, and make labor understand on the morrow the necessities imposed upon capital?

The working class has hardly consented until now to listen to any but the men who preached war and hatred. Is it truly ignorance or simplicity to imagine that it can be otherwise in the future, and that instructed, on the one side, by sad and too numerous experiences, calmed on the other, by satisfaction which the law has already given, and by that which it may still accord to its most just claims, it would wish to lend also now an attentive ear to men of good will who will recommend to it the forgetting of hatred of classes, social reconciliation, legal and pacific pursuit of means for ameliorating its condition?

Such are the questions which we modestly submit to our readers, on whatever round of the social ladder the chance of birth or their work has placed them. There are no problems more interesting; there are none which it is more necessary to solve.

The inveterate enemies of all the ideas upon which modern civilization reposes, are doubtless not as strong as they boast themselves to be, or especially as they believed not long ago ; but they are still strong and formidable. The mental malady to which a part of the Paris population is a prey, rages also in all Europe, and if we need not fear the final triumph of the social revolution, all the large cities may at least become, one day or another, the theatre of events as tragic as those which have nearly caused the total ruin of Paris. This is a danger to which we cannot too much call public attention. War is declared against civilization in all points of our old world. Everywhere the barbarians are at our gates. We must put ourselves in position to repulse their assault, on whatever spot it may be made. But let us remember that every blow given for liberty, far from weakening the enemies of social order, will only fortify them, by permitting them to disguise themselves as defenders of these sacred rights of which they have, on the contrary, just shown themselves as the most cruel and most implacable adversaries.

www.ingramcontent.com/pod-product-compliance
Lightning Source LLC
LaVergne TN
LVHW010237110826
845151LV00004B/1323
9781425524548